"Moses found he couldn't handle the crowds of Israelites in the wilderness, and many pastors know exactly how he felt! Fortunately his father-in-law helped him out. Dr. Steinbron has done the same thing for us."

—D. Stuart Briscoe

CAN THE PASTOR DO IT ALONE?

A MODEL FOR PREPARING LAY PEOPLE FOR LAY PASTORING

MELVIN J. STEINBRON

FOREWORD BY LYLE E. SCHALLER

Regal Books

A Division of GL Publications
Ventura, California, U.S.A.

Published by Regal Books
A Division of GL Publications
Ventura, California 93006
Printed in U.S.A.

Library of Congress cataloging-in-publication data applied for.

1 2 3 4 5 6 7 8 9 10 / 91 90 89 88 87 86

Rights for publishing this book in other languages are contracted by Gospel
Literature International (GLINT) foundation. GLINT also provides technical
help for the adaptation, translation, and publishing of Bible study resources
and books in scores of languages worldwide. For further information, contact
GLINT, Post Office Box 488, Rosemead, California 91770, U.S.A., or the
publisher.

Contents

Foreword

The past 35 years have brought the word *enabler* into disrepute among both lay leaders and denominational officials. For many it has become a synonym for *lazy* as the self-identified enabler passively waited for the laity to accept larger responsibilities in "running the church" or in doing the work of ministry.

This refreshing volume brings three distinctive ideas to this ancient and honorable goal of equipping the saints.

First, it recognizes this requires an active leadership role by the ordained ministry in encouraging and equipping the laity. The role of equipper is a demanding responsibility that requires vision, work, planning, persistence and confidence. It is not a passive role.

Second, the author spells out in helpful detail how to go about the process of equipping the laity for ministry.

Third, and perhaps most important, the focus is on enabling the laity to serve as pastors, not simply in administrative roles. The church exists for ministry, not administration, and this is an important distinction. This volume explains both why that is vital to the health of a redemptive worshipping community and, also, how that can be a powerful force in the spiritual growth of those who are equipped for ministry.

This may be the best book in print on how to help the laity serve as pastors in the local church.

Lyle E. Schaller

Preface

"Mel, if this program works you'll be out of a job!" A fellow clergyman made this prediction as his way of saying, "This Lay Pastors Ministry you are developing will never work. Lay people can do a lot of things, but they cannot pastor. That job is for the clergy!"

However, for eight years an increasing number of lay people have been pastoring the members of College Hill Presbyterian Church (CHPC) in Cincinnati, Ohio. In September 1978, we conducted a pilot project in which five lay people each began pastoring five to ten families. Since then, the number of lay pastors has grown to 85 pastoring units (131 individuals) pastoring 500 of our families. Our goal from the beginning was to provide adequate pastoral care for every member of CHPC by calling forth and equipping lay people gifted by the Holy Spirit for pastoring.

It has been an exciting experience for us who have developed this ministry. The excitement has not been without problems, disappointments, struggles and a lot of hard work. However, the effectiveness of the pastoring makes it all worthwhile.

11

We have been privileged in every Equipping Seminar, where we train lay people to be pastors, to include clergy and lay people representing several denominations, many states and Canada. Several churches have used our Equipping Manual and/or our video tapes and have adopted or adapted our model. This model is proving itself in small churches, as well as large.

After being approached by the publishers to write this book, I re-examined others I have read on lay people pastoring. I analyzed them, searching for what I might have to add. My conclusion was that among all the others, this book would have a unique and significant contribution to make to churches considering giving the pastoral care of their members to the laity. I saw that it would also have value for seminary use when professors want to teach future pastors how to equip their members to give pastoral care.

Here are the findings that make me believe this book is needed:

1. Persuasive appeals made to clergy and laity to share pastoring lack a practical structure by which such sharing can become one of the ministries of the Church.
2. Existing programs direct the pastoring to people in crisis or special needs, but do not include the whole congregation on a continuing basis.
3. Excellent theory, theology and principles are articulately set forth, but either they are not working or they are without a viable model to demonstrate how they will work.
4. Many attempted pastoring plans, which

have been started only to fail, leave painful frustrations, heavy guilt and fixed skepticism about lay people pastoring.

On the other hand:

1. CHPC has a Lay Pastors Ministry that is working! Its eight-year track record testifies to the strong probability of its working into the future.
2. Our ministry is *comprehensive* in that it recognizes that all people need to be pastored on a continuing basis. We all have needs. We all need someone praying for us. We all need nurturing and love.
3. Because the model we have developed has been successfully adopted or adapted by other churches, large and small, it has proven itself to be a *transferrable* model.

Compared to the other excellent books on this topic, I would not call this a how-to book, but rather a "how-it's-being-done-and-you-can-do-it-too" book. It tells the story of how *lay people are pastoring*. Now, look with me at those last four words as I place emphasis on each.

LAY PEOPLE ARE *PASTORING*

Lay people have been teaching, evangelizing, preaching and doing cross-cultural missions for decades. Why not pastoring? Just within the last two decades, God has been doing something new in the Church. He has been raising up new ministries in the United States and throughout the world, awakening lay people to the fact that they have gifts for pastoring.

The ordained clergy do not have a corner on pastoring! Lay people also have been gifted and called by the Holy Spirit. Lay people have been caring for others for centuries. But since the Church has not understood their caring to be real pastoring, it has not provided a structure for the effective use of their God-given pastoral gifts. My definition of pastoring and what activities constitute pastoring are clearly spelled out in the pages of this book.

LAY PEOPLE *ARE* PASTORING

In CHPC, lay people have been doing authentic and effective pastoring for these eight years, within the structure we call the Lay Pastors Ministry. Lay pastors are also "tending the flock" in Second Presbyterian Church in Kansas City, Missouri; Westminster Presbyterian Church in Grand Rapids, Michigan; Cedar Springs Presbyterian Church in Knoxville, Tennessee; Bethel Lutheran Church in Bellbrook, Ohio; First Presbyterian Church in Atlanta, Georgia; Chapel Rock Christian Church in Indianapolis, Indiana; Truro Episcopal Church in Washington, D.C. and other churches that have adopted or adapted the model described in this book. The number of years we have had this ministry going, along with the experience of other churches, is a strong recommendation to clergy and lay leaders alike who want to adequately care for their people.

LAY PEOPLE ARE PASTORING

When I was doing my Doctor of Ministry program with this focus, one member of the peer group, an ordained clergy from another communion, seriously questioned the right to identify a lay person as pastor. He could see them as care givers, pastors' assistants, volunteers in ministry or some other designation, but pastors? No! That title, he maintained, is to be reserved for the ordained clergy. However, if commissioned lay people *love* like pastors, *care* like pastors, *visit* like pastors, have pastoring *gifts* like pastors and *pastor* like pastors, they *are* pastors.

We have discovered that, indeed, lay people can pastor. In fact, we have discovered that often lay people's pastoring gifts are stronger than those of many ordained clergy. Lay people, gifted by the Spirit of God, called into pastoring, given authority by the laying on of hands by the elders, are authentically and effectively pastoring.

Drs. Jerry R. Kirk and Ronald R. Rand, co-pastors of CHPC, along with a staff of eight others and a committed body of elders, believe the Spirit of God has called this church to be an Equipping Center. Our Lay Pastors Ministry has drawn national attention. Two of our other ministries—*Evangelism,* with its Helper Clinic, developed by Dr. Rand, and *Christian Discipleship,* with its Counseling with Power Clinic, developed by Dr. Gary R. Sweeten— have drawn international attention as well. We equip our own people for these ministries and have equipped pastors and lay people from hundreds of other churches in these ministries. To maintain our Christian integrity as an Equipping Center, we take to heart Luke 12:48, "To whom much is given, of him will much be required."

God has given us much! His grace is abundant! In equipping others and in passing on knowledge of this ministry to you we are trying to discharge what God is requiring of us as an Equipping Center. And while equipping others, we try to keep learning. Therefore, we invite comments and suggestions from Christian brothers and sisters who read this book. And we seek counsel from churches who have similar or different ways of pastorally caring for their people.

Acknowledgments

I have not written this book without substantial help. I am indebted to Judy Jarrell for significant improvement in the content, as well as for typing and retyping the manuscript; to Marge Miller for her valuable suggestions and help in the organization of the book; Marge has worked with me in Pastoral Ministries for 10 years, first as secretary, then ministry assistant and now as pastoral assistant; to Jan Shanley, Thelma Renner, Betty Trautman, Mary Beth Bosman and others who helped with the typing (no one knows how many hundreds of pages of typing have been done, redone and scrapped in the process); to the reviewers who were honest in their criticisms: Rev. Gale Watkins, Rev. Tom Parrish, David Hodapp and Marge Miller; to the Lay Pastors Ministry Group who prayed for me; and to my wife Char who kept encouraging me and who patiently put up with less time together for over a year.

This ministry would have never taken shape and, therefore, would be nothing to write about without the commitment and creativity of the Lay Pastors Ministry

Group. Originally these were Tom and Ruth Harris, Lillard and Arlene Evans, Charles and Doris Marsh, Keith and Ann Kintner, Bob and Carole Worth, David and Pat Kuyper, Pam Helscher, Dr. Jerry and Patty Kirk, Char Steinbron and me.

The years have seen the death of one, Charles Marsh, the withdrawing of several into other ministries and the addition of Roy (Scooter) and Maren Franks, Jim and Marge Miller, Mike and Priscilla Devaney, Otto and Judy Jarrell, Geneva Grant and Nellie Pratt. We are truly partners in ministry.

Introduction

"God is always up to something," a listener commented when I told him of my personal journey from where I was in my ministry to where I felt I should be. Thus begins the story of my struggle to move from theology and theory to practice.

For the first 30 years of my ministry, I knew the biblical teaching of Ephesians 4:11,12 regarding lay people being equipped for ministry, but I did very little with it. Then things suddenly began to change.

In January 1976, I obeyed my inner drive (which I attribute to the Holy Spirit) to activate my theology. I began to lay plans for opening significant ministry to the members of the church I was then pastoring—the 400 people of Randolph Heights Presbyterian Church in St. Paul, Minnesota.

Ten months later I was called to the 2,200-member College Hill Presbyterian Church (CHPC) in Cincinnati, Ohio, as Minister of Pastoral Care. This took me from a long overdue start and instantly catapulted me in a place where I was expected to equip lay people for ministry.

The call read, "to do pastoral work and to equip lay people for pastoral work." It was the second part, "equip lay people for pastoral work," which caught my spirit and led me to accept the call. My personal commitment to the biblical teaching regarding equipping the saints for ministry, and CHPC's expectation for my doing this, has led me into the best years of my pastoring career.

GETTING FROM HERE TO THERE

It is not always easy for any of us to get from where we are to where we want to be. This is true in finances, education, social graces and every other life endeavor. It is also true of the pastoral journey, getting from the "lone ranger" style of pastoring to a shared pastoring style.

Little did I realize when I came to CHPC in November 1976 that the new direction my ministry had taken in St. Paul was really God preparing me for this dramatic change of ministry focus. While I had been reading books about lay people discovering their gifts for ministry and praying earnestly about my role as pastor-teacher-equipper, God was moving me to act on what I already believed: I should be equipping lay people to do ministry. In essence what God was saying to me was, "Mel, your 'lone ranger' way of pastoring is not doing it. Let's try it my way."

While still in St. Paul, I did three things: (1) From Easter to Pentecost I preached on the subject of lay people being gifted by the Holy Spirit for ministry; (2)I taught a class Sunday mornings on lay ministry; and (3) I made the books I had been reading available to people by purchasing additional copies for them to borrow or buy.

I was feeling a new excitement from their enthusiasm over the new growth they were experiencing. What they were feeling in their spirits was generated at the point where the inner confirmation of the Holy Spirit intersected my teaching and preaching.

However, God's purpose in igniting my spirit so as to move me toward where I should be—giving away ministry to lay people and equipping them to do it—was to get me in shape for a church that was already quite mature in equipping lay people for ministry. I began this new role in November 1976.

EQUIPPING AND LEARNING

The call to CHPC brought me into a place where I began to equip lay people for pastoring—people open to be equipped. Hundreds of lay people were already doing significant ministries such as evangelism, adult education and counseling, in addition to the traditional ministries of music, children, youth and stewardship.

These 10 years have been a constant challenge to me. Not only have I grown (and continue to grow) in my own pastoral skills, but also I have grown in the skills of equipping lay people. I have had to learn to depend upon the Lord and my colleagues, because much of the time I have been in over my head.

I have learned so much from the lay people also. They have wisdom, insights and perspectives that we professional clergy do not, much of which complement our own wisdom, insights and perspectives. Their practical understandings and methods are imperative to the functioning of our theological and "ivory tower" approaches.

WHAT A JOY!

In this new form of ministry, I have been able to "serve the LORD with gladness" (Ps. 100:2) in new ways, because

I no longer have to bear the burden of ministry alone, nor wrestle with the problems myself. Now there are many equally committed and "called" people to share the heartaches and joys of the church members.

Because of the growing number of lay people pastoring, I find I am having to do more and more planning, administrating and supporting and less and less pastoring. But what a joy! Seeing people in significant ministry, and knowing people are being cared for more like God intends, gives great satisfaction and fulfillment.

As I see it, there are four phases to my journey:

1. *Lone Ranger.* Doing all the pastoring myself, trying to be a superstar, I neglected many people because of time and energy limitations; I had failed.
2. *Calling People to Ministry Without Providing Structure.* Although I was preaching and teaching the theology of lay ministry (calling people to discover their gifts), I didn't provide the necessary discipling, or provide the necessary structures for them to be able to minister.
3. *Providing Structures.* I began to practice what I was preaching (learning from others). I began to create equipping opportunities and develop structures to follow.
4. *Continuing to Grow.* I have grown in equipping skills and have learned about working with lay people as equals.

My journey has been neither rapid nor easy. My former "lone ranger" ministry style gives way stubbornly to the new. I have discovered that I revert to the former style rapidly if I am not careful.

Because of what I am experiencing in this journey, from where I was to where I need to be, I enthusiastically endorse the following four principles formulated by one whom I call a "super pastor," Dr. Jerry Kirk, co-pastor of CHPC:

1. The pastor must become convinced that equipping lay people is God's call and priority for his ministry.
2. The pastor tastes how wonderful it is to be used by God. He sees what happens when lay people get a taste of God touching another through him.
3. The pastor must be sincere in this priority because only then will he be able to convince the congregation that he is not seeking to dodge his responsibilities but to provide better care in the long run.
4. The pastor must lead the congregation to give and receive ministry from one another. He models this by receiving ministry from the laity: their prayers, care, counsel, correction and encouragement.

THE PAY-OFF

I am finding the benefits of this journey to be many:

1. An exhilarating sense of doing things God's way.
2. An increasing impact of my ministry—

23

touching more people more deeply by multi-plication rather than by addition.

3. A lessening of the weight of the ministry—it now rests on many shoulders rather than on mine alone. God never intended that I have all the gifts needed by His people. Scripture clearly teaches that every Christian is gifted. Releasing those gifts spreads the caring responsibility across the congregation and reduces my load.

4. A continuing spiritual growth. Since we equip more by what we are than by what we teach, the process of equipping others impacts me, calling me to greater accountability and dependence upon God.

5. A reduced danger of burn-out and family alienation. Sharing the pastoring provides more time to be with my family without neglecting people, more time to be human and to lead a more balanced life.

My personal journey from where I was to where I felt I should be has been possible, first, because God has gifted many lay people for pastoring and, second, because lay people seek fulfillment in their lives through actively caring for other people.

1

Can Lay People Really Pastor?

M ommy, I'm afraid! I'm afraid!" cried the little girl who was awakened in the middle of the night by the storm. The rain beating against the window frightened her; the lightning and thunder terrified her. "Mommy, where are you! Where are you!"

Her mother hurried into her room. She sat on the side of the bed and held her daughter tightly to comfort her. Wanting to take advantage of this teachable moment, she said, "Honey, when you are frightened like this you can know that God is with you and loves you."

"Yes, Mommy, I know that," she sobbed. "But I need love with skin on."

WE ALL STRUGGLE

One of the struggles every pastor faces is how he can help his people personally and directly experience the love of God. We began to realize some years ago that there was no way we could build a staff large enough to put "love with skin on" for every one of our members if we continued to proceed in the traditional way.

As we studied the Scriptures, we discovered that there is a God-given method by which His love could be given concretely, specifically and continually to all of our members. That method is through raising up a sizable team of lay people who can be called forth, trained, equipped and then commissioned to that task—to be pastors.

The seminary-trained pastors are to be identified as those in Ephesians 4:11,12 whose call from God is to equip the saints for ministry. Equipping lay people for ministry is God's plan for the pastoral care of His people.

THEY ARE DOING IT

When we reach the end of this chapter, we shall also have reached the conclusion that lay people *can* really pastor. Our experience of lay people pastoring assigned families over the past eight years answers the question, "Can lay people really pastor?" *Yes! They are doing it! Authentically and effectively!*

"I remember getting a call from George Becker telling me Charles Fisher had just died," relates Dr. Jerry Kirk, co-pastor of CHPC. "Charles Fisher had been the superintendent of our Sunday School. He had been an elder in this church. But George Becker had been the Fisher's lay pastor. Over a period of months when Charlie Fisher was failing, George visited him regularly. He was God's 'love with skin on.' When her husband died, Mrs. Fisher called George Becker before she called me. And it was her lay pastor, George, who called me about his death.

"I remember some months ago on the way home,

stopping to visit a family who had just come home from the hospital with a new baby. When I entered the home to be with them, they said, 'Oh, our lay pastor has already been here.' Then they began to tell me what that had meant to them.

"I know of a lay pastor who had been to the hospital *daily*, ministering, and was present when the husband died. Again, I learned about the death through the lay pastor.

"I know of another situation of lay pastors helping Mrs. Tucker decide to move into a home for the elderly when it became clear that she could no longer continue in her private home."

WHAT DOES IT MEAN TO THE CLERGY?

"What does it mean to a pastor to know that scores of his people are reaching out: visiting, praying, contacting, nurturing . . . his people?" Jerry asks. Then he answers his own question: "For me it means freedom; it means gratitude; it means the sense of shared ministry that brings strength and blessing to God's people."[1]

"LOVE WITH SKIN ON"

Lay people can be the "love with skin on." The power of that kind of love is demonstrated in the following examples.

One lay pastor, a widow, requested that her flock of five to ten people be widows. One of her flock was still grieving over her husband's death and had not been in church for three years. Her husband had never been active in the church; her participation was minimal. Sadly, through all this time of sickness, death and grieving, her church had neglected her. Her busy professional pastors did not have time to care for her. However, lay pastoring has brought her into regular worship attendance and a volunteer position in one of our church offices.

For three years, one of our church families who have a 30-year-old retarded son were completely inactive and alienated from the church. They were deeply hurt by the inability of their large church to give the care they rightfully expected. Dorothy Smith became their lay pastor in November 1983. As a result, she was able to write in her April 1984 report, "A big PTL [Praise the Lord]! The Whipple family attended CHPC two times this month and is planning to be in church on Resurrection Sunday." Now these people are in church regularly; the mother plans to get involved in ministry. And as of this writing, the lay pastor thinks she has found a man to befriend the retarded son.

Another lay pastor was given a flock of people chosen at random, but living in the same general area. Late one night, one of the flock called the lay pastor, rather than a member of our pastoral staff, requesting he pray for his young son who had become suddenly ill. Over the phone the lay pastor prayed for both the son and the parents. Even though the flock member has entered the professional ministry as a Christian counselor in a nearby church, this pastoring relationship continues to this day.

The husband and wife of another family made it clear to their lay pastors (a married couple) they did not need them. However, within two weeks the husband had a heart attack. Did his wife call a member of our church staff? No, she called the lay pastors, whom they had earlier rejected.

IDENTIFY PEOPLE WITH PASTORAL GIFTS

Our church is not unique. There are lay people like these in every church who are gifted for caring, capable of loving, available to "be there" and perhaps even waiting to be called into this kind of ministry. Every observant pastor will be able to identify members of the congregation who are already caring for people. They are the ones to call together in developing a Lay Pastors Ministry, thereby making possible for all people who are pastorally gifted and available the opportunity to engage in this significant ministry.

The Scriptures do not restrict pastoring to the ordained clergy. Peter was not an installed pastor. Yet, Jesus told him, "Tend my sheep" (John 21:16). True, he had been with Jesus for nearly four years, but many church members have been "with Him" longer than that.

The elders to whom Peter gave this charge, "Tend the flock of God that is your charge" (1 Pet. 5:2), were not people with seminary degrees. The Corinthian Christians to whom Paul wrote the following words were not trained professionals: "To *each* is given the manifestation of the Spirit for the common good" (1 Cor. 12:7).[2]

THE PRESENT-DAY RENEWAL

The Scriptures not only open pastoring as a ministry for lay people, but actually call them into it. The clergy-dominated Church came near freeing lay people for this ministry in the Reformation by proclaiming the "Priesthood of Believers." However, this principle proved to be only a slogan. It did not come to life until 400-plus years later when God began raising up many programs to equip lay people for ministries, such as pastoring, which previously the clergy had kept to themselves. In the sixteenth century Reformation, the Church gave the *Scriptures* to the laity; in the present-day renewal, the Church is giving the *ministry* to the laity. What a challenge it is to be participating!

STUBBORN RESISTANCE

The centuries-long traditional role of the clergy and laity (the clergy doing the pastoring and the laity receiving it) is woefully inadequate to care for the people in our churches today. Yet, to open the pastoring ministry to lay people by developing a structure for them meets with stubborn resistance, fortified by centuries of deeply embedded practice. The resistance is threefold:

1. The *clergy* resist because they find it threatening ("I am the pastor.").
2. The *laity* resist because they feel neither capable nor worthy ("Who am I to pastor another?").
3. The *membership* resist because they pay the pastor to do this, and besides, "he's the one who is called" ("When I'm sick or need counsel, I want a real pastor.").

We have found, however, that this resistance is not strong enough to hold out against the pastoral care given faithfully by gifted, equipped and commissioned lay people. Lacking the advantage of acceptance because of seminary training and ordination, lay people quickly earn acceptance as pastors by *doing* it.

ASSUMPTIONS PROVED

"Lay people can pastor," and "members will accept pastoring from lay people" were two of our assumptions when we began to develop our Lay Pastors Ministry. Reports from our lay pastors consistently prove these assumptions to be true.

To develop this ministry, we called together 15 lay people to work together with one of the other pastors and me. We called this a "Ministry Group."

We decided to do a pilot project to test our assumptions. We needed to put this ministry together by field experience as well as armchair planning. The pilot project was to last six months. Five members of the Ministry Group volunteered to pastor five to ten families for that time.

The first to report on his home visits was Charles Marsh: "I had no trouble arranging the visit. The Petersons were glad to have me come, even though they didn't know me and I don't recall ever having seen them before. We talked about their family, his job and the weather. I told them about the Lay Pastors Ministry."

I could tell by the tone of his voice, the look in his eyes and his earnestness that Charles was as turned on to pastoring as I was. He continued, "These two were ready to leave the church. They felt unnoticed by the staff and others. They objected to some things about the preaching. We talked about these things. I assured them that I would report their objections to the preaching staff. They felt good about our getting together in another two or three weeks. We prayed before I left. I can hardly wait to get together with that young couple again!"

The follow-up to this report is that the Petersons not

only renewed their commitment to the church, but two years later became lay pastors themselves.

For Charles, the six-month pilot project stretched to seven years. Only his death severed the relationships he had developed during his lay pastoring years.

Do we need to ask, "Can lay people really pastor?"

LISTEN TO THE EXPERTS

Much recent study confirms the effectiveness of lay people in the role of helper. Psychologist Robert Carkuff's research shows that lay people can learn to help as effectively as professional helpers. For many purposes and problems, lay people can be as effective or more effective than credentialed helpers. Lay people can learn to understand others and act upon this understanding as well as or better than professionals.[3]

Many lay people have these three qualities and will bring them into their pastoring relationships:

1. Accurate empathic understanding
2. Unconditional positive warmth
3. Genuineness.[4]

Two statements I read years ago, which I have reflected upon and repeated to others often, helped me to believe that lay people can truly pastor:

>   *One.* Oscar E. Feucht's definition of a church: "A ministerium of all who have Christ in their hearts."[5]
>   *Two.* Samuel Southard's bold position:

"Many persons can do most of what we pastors
do . . . . The task of pastors is to equip these
persons for ministry and support them through
administration and example."[6]

THE PASTORHOOD OF BELIEVERS

Alastair Campbell, a Scottish churchman and theologian, is a firm believer in what he calls "the pastorhood of all believers." I love what he says in his book *Rediscovering Pastoral Care:*

Pastoral care . . . is not correctly understood if
it is viewed within the framework of professionalism . . . . Pastoral care is a relationship
founded upon the integrity of the individual.
Such a relationship does not depend primarily
upon the acquisition of knowledge or the development of skill. Rather, it depends upon a caring attitude toward others which comes from
our own experience of pain, fears, and loss, and
our own release from their deadening grip.[7]

Following this, Campbell uses the term "enfleshed
love"[8] to refer to the caring person. Our lay pastors have
been this "enfleshed love" to hundreds of people for whom
the professional staff could not have been available, and
who would have therefore been neglected. We believe in
the "pastorhood of believers," because we see it working!

The governing board of our church, the Session,
believes in it too. In 1978, they took official action to adopt
the Lay Pastors Ministry as the way this church will now
pastor its people.

IT'S NOT THAT DIFFICULT

What I am finding, from the pastoring our lay people are doing and from the books I continue to read on this topic, is that pastoring is not all that difficult. Kenneth R. Mitchell and Herbert Anderson, experts in dealing with losses and grief, list in their book *All Our Losses, All Our Griefs* aspects common to all caring:

> Simply standing by as a listening presence comfortable with silence; bearing with individuals in their pain and confusion; responding encouragingly when strong feelings are expressed; and lending strength to people when they need an emotional prop.[9]

Besides possessing those aspects, which are common to both laity and clergy, lay people are generally more available to the person who needs the caring attention, the "enfleshed love."

I discovered that a lot of confidence is invested in lay people by the authors of *Taking Time,* a publication by the United States Department of Health and Human Services:

> The person with cancer needs family or friends as a constant in a changing world. "I am here," offers great reserves of support.[10]

If our government has this confidence in lay people, the Church ought not to doubt the ability of its lay people to pastor others. How dare we think that only the clergy can be pastors! At CHPC, we trust our lay people. That trust is warranted as they are proving again and again that a lay person is able to be the friend and, therefore, the "constant in a changing world." They also are likely to be available to say "I am here" more frequently than the professional clergy.

In my reading, I have identified the following essential qualities for pastoring: empathy, warmth, genuineness, integrity, caring attitude, listening, availability, bearing with and the ability to encourage.

It is clear that these primary qualifications for giving pastoral care are neither limited to professionals nor are they acquired through degree programs. They are gifts of God to both lay and professional pastors that can be identified and nurtured into powerful caring skills. That lay people have these qualities validates one of the assumptions made when we began to develop this ministry: Lay people can pastor.

WILL CHURCH MEMBERS ACCEPT
LAY PASTORING?

Will lay people accept pastoring from their peers? The ability and readiness of lay people to pastor must be met by the readiness of other lay people to accept them as pastors if, indeed, pastoring is to take place. Again, our experience says, "Yes! They will." However, honesty compels me to level with you and admit to a few exceptions.

Yet, these exceptions also make it fair to ask, "Do lay people always accept the pastoring of the professional?" As every ordained pastor knows, there are some people who will contribute to the budget and occasionally attend the worship services, while at the same time resist a visit from the professional pastor. My point is that the very few who are not open to receiving a lay pastor in no way invalidates our assumption that members will accept the pastoring offered by called, equipped and commissioned lay people. They are doing it, in our church and many other churches!

Dr. Kenneth Haugk is the founder of the Stephen Series system of training and organizing lay persons for caring ministry in and around their congregations. When asked, "Will people who need care really accept the ministry of lay persons?" he responds with a resounding, Yes!

> Ninety percent or more of the time, "helpees"
> willingly accept visitation by a Stephen minister.
> The key is that the "helpees" need to be properly prepared for Stephen ministry to them.[11]

So, we come to the conclusion we knew we would reach when we started this chapter: Lay people can really pastor! We have, however, been able to reach this conclusion only because God planned it this way. The next chapter shows that this conclusion is rooted in the Bible.

Notes:

1. This story is told by Dr. Jerry Kirk in our Lay Pastors Equipping video tapes. The tapes are available from Pastoral Ministries, College Hill Presbyterian Church, 5742 Hamilton Ave., Cincinnati, OH 45224. Phone: (513) 541-5676.
2. From this reference onwards, all italicized words and phrases in Scripture quotations are added by the author for emphasis and clarification.
3. Cited by Dr. Gary Sweeten in his doctoral dissertation, "The Development of a Systematic Human Relations Training Model for Evangelical Christians," (Ed. D. dissertation, University of Cincinnati, 1975), p. 135.

4. Samuel Southard, *Training Church Members for Pastoral Care* (Valley Forge, PA: Judson Press, 1982), p. 76.
5. Oscar E. Feucht, *Everyone a Minister* (St. Louis, MO: Concordia Publishing House, 1974), p. 8.
6. Samuel Southard, *Comprehensive Pastoral Care* (Valley Forge, PA: Judson Press, 1975), p. 7.
7. Alastair Campbell, *Rediscovering Pastoral Care* (Philadelphia, PA: Westminster Press, 1981), p. 41.
8. Ibid., pp. 46, 47.
9. Kenneth R. Mitchell and Herbert Anderson, *All Our Losses, All Our Griefs* (Philadelphia: Westminster Press, 1983), p. 117.
10. From *Taking Time* (Support for People with Cancer and the People Who Care About Them), Publication of the United States Department of Health and Human Services, Office of Cancer Communications, National Cancer Institute, Bethesda, MD 20205, p. 28.
11. The Stephen Series is one good example of a thorough and well-organized system for putting into practice the basic concept of this book. It encompasses the organization, administration, training and supervision of lay people in pastoral care. More information can be obtained by contacting Stephen Ministries, 1325 Boland, St. Louis, MO 63117. Phone (314) 645-5511.

2

It's in the Book

God said it! I believe it! That settles it!" Bumper-sticker faith is not always reliable, but this one certainly is. How dare anyone doubt that lay people are to pastor when God speaks so clearly. His Scripture:

1. Reveals the concept
2. Calls us to care for one another
3. Teaches that His Spirit gives pastoring gifts to believers
4. Provides models for caring for His people.

So far I have done a lot of talking about pastoring. It's time to define what I mean. Pastoring is: *caring for another by giving one's self in Christian love to a relationship in times of weakness and times of strength*. My definition assumes the following: everybody needs another who cares for him or her; the strength of caring is in the relationship; Christian love is a giving love; and, people need somebody who cares for them consistently, both when they are in need and when all is well.

THE FIRST LAY PASTORS

The concept of lay pastoring originates in the Scriptures. Peter was still a fisherman at heart when Jesus called to him: "Take care of my sheep" (John 21:16, *NIV*). He had gone back to fishing after Jesus' death and resurrection. The elders whom Peter pressed into pastoring with the words, "Be shepherds of God's flock that is under your care" (1 Pet. 5:2, *NIV*), were not formally schooled for pastoring. When Paul wrote to the "saints" at Ephesus to instruct them that every one of them was given gifts for ministry, gifts that were to be enhanced and directed by pastor-teachers, he was writing to people who had no professionally designated role (see Eph. 4:7-12).

GOD CALLS LAY PEOPLE TO PASTOR

The conclusion from these and other Scriptures is that lay people not only *may* be pastors if they choose, but also *are called* to be authentic and effective pastors. Samuel Southard supports this conclusion when he writes, "Many persons can do most of what we pastors can do; our special task as pastors is to prepare others for service and support them both through administration and example in that service.[1]

Southard becomes specific when he says, "The priorities of a pastor's services are reversed in this system. Instead of going first to the sick and the lonely, the pastor will spend most of the time and attention with the healthy members who then become ministers to the sick and lonely."[2]

God calls us to care for His people. He calls to us as He

40

did to Isaiah, "Comfort, comfort my people" (Isa. 40:1). The word *comfort* comes from two Latin words, *con* and *fortis,* meaning "strengthen by being with." What a description of pastoring!

God does not want people in our churches to lament as the psalmist did, "There is none who takes notice of me ... no man cares for me" (Ps. 142:4). How many people in our churches today cry this in one form or another because the professional pastor is the only one pastoring. People are neglected because we are not pastoring God's way, which is equipping lay people He has called to tend His flock.

Part of what Jesus intended when He said to His disciples on the evening of the day of His resurrection, "As the Father has sent me, even so I send you" (John 20:21), is that His disciples of our day are to pastor like He did—caring, helping, accepting, healing, comforting, assuring, confronting, being with and interceding.

The need for structuring pastoral care so as to be certain no one will "fall through the cracks" is suggested in Jesus' parable of the one lost sheep. It concludes with this strong admonition: "So it is not the will of my Father who is in heaven that one of these little ones should perish" (Matt. 18:14).

Is the professional shepherd-pastor who neglects his people (not willfully, but because he is trying to do it alone) any less "worthless" than those whom Zechariah accuses of deserting the flock, "A shepherd who does not care for the perishing, or seek the wandering, or heal the maimed, or nourish the sound" (Zech. 11:16). The end result is the same whether by willful neglect or neglect by default—God's people are not being shepherded.

41

MOSES HAD TO LEARN

Moses, great leader that he was, was not adequately caring for God's people. When his father-in-law Jethro observed that Moses was exhausting himself in trying to hear and help all the people and yet so many of them were neither heard nor helped, he said to Moses, "What you are doing is not good" (Exod. 18:17). Here is where we find one biblical model for our Lay Pastors Ministry. In this model we see:

1. The traditional way of one person trying to minister to all the people is not adequate: "You are not able to perform it alone," and "the thing is too heavy for you" (Exod. 18:18).

2. The people will not know what to do unless they are equipped: "You shall teach them . . . what they must do" (v. 20).

3. There are qualifications for those who are to pastor: "Choose able men from all the people . . . men who are trustworthy" (v. 21).

4. The structure was simple: "Place such men over the people as rulers of thousands, of hundreds, of fifties, and of tens" (v. 21). This gets the caring down to "bite-size."

5. The plan was specific: "Let them judge the people at all times" (v. 22). They were to decide on certain matters. The greater matters they were to bring to Moses.

6. The results were spectacular:
   (a) "It will be easier for you" (v. 22).
   (b) "They will bear the burden with you" (v. 22).

(c) "You will be able to endure" (v. 23).

(d) "This people also will go to their place in peace" (v. 23).

Moses' greatness is seen in being honest and humble enough to accept his father-in-law's counsel. He lost no time in implementing it. I am sure that being "pressed to the wall" helped him to be honest and humble, and to take action.

Another model is found in the book of Numbers. Moses complained to God, "I am not able to carry all this people alone, the burden is too heavy for me" (Num. 11:14). How many clergy are like this? Moses' desperation opened him to hearing God's plan to choose 70 elders to bear the burden of the people with him that he might not bear it alone.

Like Moses, I cried out to God many times before I began my journey from where I was to where I needed to be. My shameful confession is that I heard God for years, but did not act upon what He was calling me to do. I kept plodding along in the traditional model, getting as much done as one man could do, proud of my fatigue and neglecting my family in the process. I was unable to pastor my people adequately, and felt the added burden of guilt for not getting it all done.

GOD GIVES HIS SPIRIT

God's way of caring for His people is so much more superior! In the Numbers' model, God told Moses, "I will take some of the spirit which is upon you and put it upon them [the elders]" (Num. 11:17). We cannot know for certain whether "spirit" is spelled with a capital S or a small

43

s—whether it is God's Spirit or Moses' spirit. In any case, today God gives His Spirit to every true believer in Jesus Christ, and this Spirit gives each one gifts for ministry, calls each one into ministry and makes each one's ministry fruitful (see 1 Cor. 12:7,11).

God's act of giving His Spirit is a large part of the biblical basis for our Lay Pastors Ministry. We know that without the Holy Spirit at work, all our efforts would be futile. The power of Pentecost is the power at work in pastoring—"You shall receive power when the Holy Spirit has come upon you" (Acts 1:8).

Jesus promised the Spirit (see John 14:16,17); Paul reveals the Spirit as the One who enables inner growth and equips the saints for ministry (see Rom. 8:9-11 and 1 Cor. 12:4-11); Luke reveals the Spirit as the One who empowers for witness and ministry (see Luke 24:48,49; Acts 1:8).

When our Ministry Group began to lay the foundation for the Lay Pastors Ministry (discussed in chapter 4), we spent considerable time studying what the Bible had to teach about pastoring. This was some of the most productive study we did because through it we became convinced that this was God's way of caring for His people. This conviction galvanized us into action and caused us to look very seriously at the needs of our people for their adequate pastoral care.

Notes:

1. Samuel Southard, *Comprehensive Pastoral Care* (Valley Forge, PA: Judson Press, 1975), p. 7.
2. Ibid., p. 6.

3

What Is Lay Pastoring and Who Needs It?

Give your name and tell one thing you would like the others to know about you. It may be something one of your children has just done, your favorite restaurant or where you like to go on vacation. You'll have eight minutes to do this."

What you have just read is part of our Lay Pastors Equipping Seminars. The registrants have been divided into groups of four; they are exchanging names and sharing some of their lives with each other.

In exactly eight minutes, we begin again, "Next, I want you to share with the other three in your group one of the following: a need you know a friend or acquaintance has; a need a member of your family has; or a need of your own. Take another eight minutes for this.

"Now, each one pray for the need one of your group shared. Pray for just one. This way all four will pray and all four will have their needs lifted to God."

When it's apparent most of the groups have finished praying, I begin to sing softly. Those finished join with me. We sing softly until all eyes are open. This is a very precious time. A certain mood of holy quietness takes over.

"Do you know what you have just done?" Silence. "You have just pastored one another." Then the "Ah-ha." They were there; they listened; they shared; they loved; they prayed.

EVERYBODY HAS NEEDS

This experience has become one of the high-energy times in our Equipping Seminars. Among other things, it reveals the fact that everybody has concerns and needs. So, who needs to be pastored? Everybody! God would have every one of His children prayed for, cared for and loved by another when life is going well, and when it is not.

Occasionally, there are those who do not want a lay pastor to call on them because they think they have no need for a pastor. Ruth, one of our lay pastors, asked me what she should do about a woman who would not allow her to come to her home for the first visit. It was eight months since she had been equipped and commissioned. She had telephoned this member of her flock several times to no avail. I suggested she go to her home uninvited and unannounced.

"Meet me at the church at two o'clock next Sunday and we'll go together," I offered. We rang the doorbell. The woman opened the door. I introduced the two of us and asked if we could come in.

"I'm busy, but come in," she said reluctantly. So far, so good. When I saw that she was busy baking, I suggested that Ruth and I wait in the living room until she was finished. I told her Ruth and I had some things to talk over anyway.

Our hostess came in shortly after and following some

pleasant small talk, she warmed up to us. She even offered us some of her freshly baked cookies. As we talked, we discovered that she had an invalid mother in the next room. She said she hired a "mother-sitter" during the day while she was at work. This meant that she was confined to her home nights and weekends to care for her mother.

We had discovered a need! She thought she had no needs that required a pastor. And Ruth, her lay pastor, had come to the erroneous conclusion that this woman did not need her because she had not responded favorably to her calls.

Upon leaving, the two women embraced, mingled tears and agreed to keep in touch. Does this have something to say to us? I believe it says that everybody has needs. Everybody needs pastoring, even though they may be reluctant to acknowledge those needs.

Someone has an invalid mother . . . a marriage is in trouble . . . he has a bad back . . . they have financial problems . . . her son is in trouble with the law . . . his mother-in-law died last week . . . these all spell *needs*.

One time when I was sitting in a circle of 30 good friends, my eyes moved systematically from one to the next as I called to mind a specific and unique need each one of them had, including myself. We were all Christians with deep commitments to Christ; we were all involved in Christian ministry; we were all in need of prayer. We all needed a pastor.

IT DOESN'T JUST HAPPEN

The program of caring must be planned. It doesn't just happen. Just as we plan other parts of the life of our churches such as education, evangelism, worship, finances and properties, we must also plan for the pastoral care of our membership.

If we just let care happen, or leave it entirely up to the clergy or those who do some pastoring on their own anyway, there will be some members of God's family who will get no care at all. Or if they do, it may be too little and/or too late.

A church must become intentional in giving pastoral care. Otherwise, many needs will go unnoticed or unmet, especially of those who are less verbal or visible. Dr. Kenneth Haugk writes:

> Congregations that wouldn't question the need for planning in order to install a new pipe organ or stained glass windows, to add persons to the church staff, or to expand a facility, often have difficulty understanding that a caring ministry requires the same thoughtful planning as other dimensions of congregational life. In fact, planning for caring should receive special attention, because the congregation's call to care for people in times of hurt or need or crisis is at the very heart of a congregation's existence and life.[1]

BUILD A RELATIONSHIP!

What about those people who don't seem to have an immediate crisis? Those who do not appear to be hurting actually may be, because everybody hurts at one time or another. That is one of life's realities.

One of our lay pastors faithfully built a relationship with a married couple when life for that couple was going well.

Suddenly, there was a crisis—a heart attack. The long and only partial recovery put such stress on the marriage that the couple separated. The lay pastor continued to pray for them and kept in touch. Because of the level of trust and confidence he had built while things were going well, the couple accepted his recommendation for counseling, and later were reconciled.

It is just as important to pastor people when there are no critical problems in their lives as when there are, for it is the relationship that is built in noncrisis times that earns the lay pastor's right to be trusted during the hurting times.

PASTORING IS ALSO NURTURING

We rarely think of spiritual nurture when we speak of needs. But it is a definite need! Pastoring should be seen as nurturing people in their lives in Christ, as well as building a relationship in noncrisis times. Adding the dimensions of nurturing and relationship-building broadens the scope of pastoring to include:

1. Building a relationship in noncrisis times
2. Caring and helping in a crisis
3. Nurturing in faith.

Whereby, some pastoring plans are only for troubled times in people's lives, withdrawing from the relationship when the trouble has passed, we perceive our Lay Pastors Ministry to be comprehensive. There are pastoring plans that are more communication focused to keep people in touch with the Church. Our model includes this purpose, but broadens itself to fully pastor a person and his family on a continuing basis. Spiritual nurture is included.

We tell our lay pastors, "When you have pastored them, they are pastored. You are not just being in touch or caring for one until the *real* pastor can get there. *You* are the real pastor!"

WHOLISTIC CARE

When the apostle Paul met with the Ephesian elders and instructed them to care for the Church of God (see Acts 20:28), he meant for them to assist people in their spiritual growth and celebrate glad times with them as well as to help them in times of trouble. When Peter called the elders of the dispersion to "tend the flock of God" (1 Pet. 5:2), he meant for them to encourage people toward Christian maturity as well as to be with them and to pray for them in times of despair. This is a type of wholistic care, a comprehensive care that we offer in our Lay Pastors Ministry.

Samuel Southard sees lay people giving this wholistic care. He writes in *Training Church Members for Pastoral Care*, "Pastoral care is a broader term that could mean counsel, if desired, but also implies oversight—a concern for people in the church *whether they have problems or not.*"[2]

Ephesians chapter 4 informs us that pastoring, "the work of the ministry," should accomplish these objectives:

1. Build up the Body of Christ.
2. Attain the unity of the faith.
3. Assist people to maturity.
4. Enable people to measure up to the "stature of the fulness of Christ."

5. Speak the truth in love.
6. Help people "to grow up in . . . Christ."
7. Help each part of the Body work properly.
8. Facilitate upbuilding in love. (See vv. 12-16.)

Does everybody need to be pastored by somebody when we see the full range of pastoring? The answer is an unequivocal, "Yes, of course."

PEOPLE NEED TO USE THEIR GIFTS

There is another group of people to consider when we ask the question, Who needs it? Those people who are gifted by the Spirit with the gifts of mercy, compassion and other pastoral gifts need to be able to *use* those gifts in pastoring activities. If they don't, they can become frustrated, unfulfilled and stunted in their spiritual maturity. Lay people are not to be denied the joy and growth we professional pastors experience in God's ministry. His intent is that our gifts be recognized and utilized fully for our sake and for the sake of the Body.

OTHER CHURCHES WILL INQUIRE

There is one more answer to the question, Who needs it? Other churches, that's who. Authentic pastoring by lay people is relatively new in the American Church, as well as the Christian Church worldwide. Because we at CHPC have a model that is working, we get inquiries from around the world. We have heard from churches throughout America. We have even heard from Canada, Australia and South Africa.

Should your church open pastoring to lay people, you will discover, as we did, that other churches will want to know what you are doing. When they see the effectiveness of your program, they will seek your help. You will be part of the new thing God is doing in our time in His Church.

A good illustration of how this program can spread is the story of the lay ministry to a mother of one of our church members who was critically ill in Chattanooga, Tennessee. Our church member went to be with her mother in the hospital, and while there was visited by a man who introduced himself as a lay pastor from Central Presbyterian Church. He was there to minister to the patient and administered to the daughter as well. A few years earlier Central Presbyterian Church had adopted our Lay Pastors Ministry.

Who needs lay pastoring? Everyone! And once we established this answer, we were led to establish the goal of providing a lay pastor for every member of our congregation. We're excited to share just how we got started.

Notes:

1. From "The Stephen Series Newsletter," Summer 1985, Stephen Ministries, 1325 Boland, St. Louis, MO 63117.
2. Samuel Southard, *Training Church Members for Pastoral Care* (Valley Forge, PA: Judson Press, 1982), p. 18.

4

Getting Started

The beginning of our Lay Pastors Ministry goes back to that time when we first became aware of the need for pastoring. People were saying members of our church were not being cared for. Cries were not being heard; hurts were not being healed.

Many personal and family problems were not given due attention. People were not being helped adequately in their social, financial, relational and employment struggles. The supportive helps of encouragement, affirmation, listening and just being there were not sufficient to match the needs.

Sometimes those in the hospital were not visited and prayed with. Several people in nursing homes and other aged and infirm people were being neglected. Even spiritual needs were not given the attention a church needs and wants to give. In short, we were not tending God's people very well.

"With the size staff we have, I don't see why at least

one of them couldn't have visited," was a common criticism.

CHURCH SIZE NOT AN ISSUE

We want to note here that both large and small churches are deluded into thinking that the other offers adequate care of members. People in large churches think members of smaller churches are adequately pastored, because the pastor has the time. People in smaller churches think members of large churches receive adequate pastoral care because the multiple staff has the time. Both are misinformed!

I have pastored small churches and am now on staff at a large church. Neither size church gives adequate pastoral care under the traditional ministry program. Modern ministry demands are so great that neither the professional pastors of smaller churches nor the professional pastors on large church staffs are able to pastor people as both they and their members would like.

Having to face the reality that many people are not being pastored is a great frustration to committed and overworked pastors. It hurts deeply to see people with needs go neglected because of time and energy limitations. Added to this frustration and hurt is burdensome guilt.

Awareness of neglected people called forth this action by our Session in May 1975: "Each committee shall be responsible for pastoring its own people . . . . The Pastoring Committee shall be responsible for all CHPC members *not* covered by a committee."

Although the intent behind this action was good it was fruitless because a more detailed plan to implement the

54

directive was not drafted. It would be like the United States Congress passing legislation for a project and then failing to appropriate the necessary funds. However, the directive did lay the foundation for the outcry of the senior pastor, "When is this Session going to do something about pastoring our people!?"

CHPC'S NEED FOR LAY PASTORING

Three of us—the chairperson of Sessions' Pastoral Ministries Committee, the senior pastor and I—began to discuss with great concern the senior pastor's remark. I need to relate at this point the reason we were able to move from being aware of the need to the actual implementation of our Lay Pastors Ministry.

Thus far, our congregation had been nurtured by preaching, precept and practice in the concept of the ministry of the laity. Such truths found in Ephesians 4, 1 Corinthians 12-14, Romans 12 and 1 Peter 4 and 5, along with the Lordship of Jesus Christ had been taught at CHPC for a number of years. Those truths include:

1. Pastor-teachers are to equip "the saints" for ministry. That is their priority call from God. It is His plan for ministry.
2. Every Christian has been given gifts for ministry. These can be identified and used in significant ministry.
3. Jesus Christ is Lord. We are to respond to His Lordship by using our gifts in ministry.

A wide acceptance of these truths from God prepared the way for the development of our Lay Pastors Ministry.

55

FROM AWARENESS TO MEETING THE NEED

Early in 1978 we formed a Ministry Group to examine our pastoral needs. A Ministry Group is formed around a specific ministry such as missions, evangelism or pastoring. Worship, *koinonia* and nurture are as integral a part of the group meetings as working on the specific ministry. Group members share their lives as well as the responsibility for their ministry.

Our ministry group was composed of 17 people. Although there were several of us, we were able to function effectively. The only members of staff were Jerry Kirk, who committed himself for one year, and I. The other 15 were lay people—selected because of their concern for pastoring—and were representative of the variety of people in our church.

After much Bible study and reading of books on the topic of pastoring, our group came up with these major aspects for which we later provided structure:

1. Qualifications of a lay pastor
2. Ministry description (What will a lay pastor do?)
3. Length of commitment
4. Calling forth (Enlisting people to be lay pastors)
5. Equipping (Basic and continuing)
6. Flocking (Assigning families to lay pastors)
7. Organizational structure
8. Supervision (by shepherds who are lay pastors of lay pastors)
9. Accountability (reports)
10. Authority (Commissioning)

11. Communication (A monthly newsletter to lay pastors and articles in the church paper)
12. Evaluation

OUR PILOT PROJECT

After a year of learning and planning, we decided to conduct a pilot project. It would run for six months to field-test our planning. That meant we were off and running.

Five members of the Ministry Group volunteered to pastor between five and ten families each for the six-month test period. During that time the five members visited their families, tested our assumptions, began building relationships and prayed for the people daily.

The pilot project proved successful. It was so successful that five years after the pilot project each one of the original five was continuing to pastor the same people they had pastored in the first six months. This unplanned continuation demonstrated the bonding of lives in an authentic pastoral relationship. It was happening!

NEXT STEP—RECRUITMENT OF OTHERS

We proceeded to recruit additional people for this ministry. At last, the need for pastoring our people effectively was beginning to be met by called, equipped, committed and commissioned lay people. It was confirmed, we were doing things according to God's design.

Now eight years later, staff members feel less harried and less guilty. Seldom do we hear even one second-hand complaint about our people being neglected. And lay people who are pastoring are being fulfilled in their spirits as never before.

DO IT TOGETHER

If you decide to begin a lay pastors ministry in your church, there is one step you must take first. You must call forth a group of lay people concerned about the church, especially about the pastoring, and begin to work on it together. The lay people must have personal ownership of the ministry and ownership comes from facing the need and developing the ministry together. The lay people have to get in on the ground floor! What is designed by the professional clergy alone in the "ivory tower" is likely to fail.

As a pastor who used the "ivory tower" approach during most of my years of ministry, I had a difficult time adjusting to the process of working closely with lay people who had equal ownership of what we were doing. But I learned, stubbornly and slowly, from their wisdom and knowledge. And they learned from my idealism, spirit and theology. Together we forged a ministry design that we owned equally. What great respect I have for the practical approaches, creative ideas, openness to learning and the committed abilities of lay people. They needed me; I needed them. We needed each other.

This need for each other is underscored by Marlene Wilson, an expert in enlisting volunteers:

> People are committed to plans they help make.
> Yet this is frequently overlooked by both clergy
> and lay leadership. So, the first principle in good
> planning is to involve those affected by the plan
> in the process.[1]

An amusing example of our needing each other is when I presented to the Ministry Group my description of what a lay pastor ought to be. I was using my old "ivory tower" approach of developing the description. I worked out what I thought was a good plan, and presented it to the group at our next meeting. Everyone took my suggestion home to study but when we met again and I pressed for acceptance, I sensed some disagreement. Finally the Ministry Group leader Tom Harris said in a firm tone, "Mel, it looks to me like you are looking for people who can walk on water and we don't have many of those."

We all laughed. But Tom had gotten his point across. I understood clearly. I was humbled (but not humiliated) by his wisdom. My lofty ideas were good, but not practical.

From that point on we have worked cooperatively to design what a lay pastor would *be* and *do*. The imperative principle is that neither the clergy nor the laity alone can design a viable ministry that will be effective and lasting. Together, however, it can be done!

GOD DOES IT

We say that God raised up this ministry at CHPC to meet the pastoring need. And He did! However, He did it like He delivered the children of Israel out of Egypt. He called Moses from the bush and said, "I have seen the affliction of my people . . . and I have come down to deliver them . . . Come, I will send *you.*" (Exod. 3:7-10). We could almost hear God say to us, "I have heard the lament of my people at CHPC and have come to pastor them. Come, I will send *you!*"

I am convinced that God is calling every church to open its ministry of pastoring to lay people. Wherever the clergy and lay people will be a team to design a way to do it—bringing the training and experience of the professional pastor together with the wisdom and practical knowledge of committed lay people—God will pastor His people. It is as Thomas Gillespie says:

> [This pastoring] will be realized only if the non-clergy are willing to move up, if the clergy are willing to move over, and if all God's people are willing to move out.[2]

PREPARING A CONGREGATION

In churches where the principle of lay people being called to authentic ministry is new—and this is a revolutionary concept to many—there is much work to be done.

Unless the leadership of the church is convinced that this principle is of God, and unless its pastor is ready to give time to preaching and teaching about God's call to lay people to be ministers, a Lay Pastors Ministry will not be accepted even if a cadre of lay pastors could be enlisted.

The whole congregation has to be prepared to give and receive lay ministry. Ways to prepare the congregation include:

1. Preach a series of sermons on the subject.
2. Hold classes to coordinate preaching, teaching, study and discussion.
3. Communicate via church paper and pastoral letters.
4. Share your actions, vision and plans with your people and invite them to be with you in action and spirit.
5. Hold "Lay Witness" renewal weeks or weekends.

6. Have selected books on gifts for ministry, lay involvement in ministry, etc. to sell and/ or borrow. (Titles in the bibliography of this book are suitable.)
7. Observe members who are already caring for others. Every church has them. Encourage them and draw their attention to their effective ministry. These people are possibilities for your Ministry Group.

THE THREE PHASES

After a few years of lay pastoring we discovered there are three phases to this ministry. They are:

Phase I Development—putting the ministry together
Phase II Implementation—getting it off the ground
Phase III Maintenance—keeping it going.

After the development phase, which took us one year to complete, all three phases continue simultaneously. For example:

Phase I. Development is continuous. From doing the ministry you learn what needs to be changed, what is working, what is not working and why. The struggles will be many, requiring study, evaluation, prayer and many meetings. The tendency is to not change the original design. We are changing constantly. Anything that is alive experiences change.

Phase II. Implementation is continuous. Some lay pastors will drop out and need to be replaced. New members will require additional lay pastors. Or, it may take a long time, perhaps a few years, to fully implement this ministry. To fully implement ours we are conducting 15-hour equipping seminars three times a year for new lay pastors.

Phase III. Maintenance is continuous. This is necessary to handle problems that may arise, modify procedures and bring lay pastors together regularly for encouragement, fellowship, equipping, evaluating and supervision.

FROM AWARENESS TO ACTION

In summary, following these seven steps will move a church from an *awareness* of the need to adequately pastor all church members to *meeting* that need:

1. Prepare the people (see page 60)
2. Call a Ministry Group together
3. Design a structure (invent, adopt or adapt)
4. Provide for the 12 aspects listed on page 56 and 57
5. Have plan adopted by official board
6. Call forth, equip and commission
7. Assign families to lay pastors.

Next we will discuss what a lay pastor does and how to go about equipping them for adequate and effective ministry.

Notes:

1. Marlene Wilson, *How to Mobilize Church Volunteers* (Minneapolis, MN: Augsburg Publishing House, 1983), p. 49.
2. Quoted by James L. Garlow in *Partners in Ministry* (Kansas City, MO: Beacon Hill Press, 1981), p. 9.

5

What a Lay Pastor Does

Exactly what does a lay pastor do?" asks one who is hearing about our Lay Pastors Ministry for the first time. We explain that we equip our lay pastors to do four things and to know that as they do these they are actually pastoring people. These four areas are easily remembered by using the acrostic *PACE*.

P - *Pray* for each one regularly.

A - Be *available*.

C - *Contact* each one on a regular basis.

E - Provide a Christian *example*.

PACE is the heart of our Lay Pastors Ministry. It constitutes basic, elementary pastoring. Tom Harris, our first ministry leader, made two practical observations about PACE:

1. If this is all the pastoring people get, it is

more than most of them are getting now.

2. When lay pastors start with these they will not quit there but will go farther.

Let's look at these four areas, one at a time.

Pray. Our Ministry Group leader, Roy Franks, says, "We have had people say, 'Don't visit me,' but we have never had one say, 'Don't pray for me.'"

We ask our lay pastors to pray daily for the people in their flock. In addition to depending upon God to answer their prayers, prayer does at least four other things:

1. It *builds a concern* on behalf of Christ for their flock.
2. It silently *builds the relationship* for it is a form of secretive contact. Lay pastors have told how their love, concern and sense of belonging have deepened over days and weeks of faithful praying.
3. It deepens their sense of *responsibility*. It gives God a chance to place the pastoring squarely on their shoulders and plant it deeply in their hearts.
4. A time of prayer is a *creative* time between God and the lay pastor in which ideas of what should be done are generated and the appropriate time and frequency for contact is determined. I believe prayer is the key to effective pastoring.

Available. On the first visit the lay pastors offer their availability in words like, "If you have some concerns you would like us to pray about, or if there are ways I can be of any use to you, please call me." They give the flock member a card with their name, address and phone number to affirm their offer. It is not uncommon at all for members of a flock, believing the availability of their lay pastors, to call on them for prayer or help.

Contact. We ask a minimum of one contact a month be made to each flock member. Within a month after being commissioned lay pastors make their first visit, a home visit, to get acquainted, to explain the ministry and to share expectations for the relationship. A letter is sent from my office informing the church members they now have a lay pastor and giving them his or her name. This helps pave the way for the first visit. After the first visit many of the contacts can be made by phone, mail or an informal chat at church on Sunday mornings. Some lay pastors invite their flock members to their homes or meet them at a restaurant.

The importance of these casual contacts is that they enable lay pastors to know when there are problems calling for more intentional and intensive pastoring activity.

In order for lay pastors to make regular contacts, the flock size is kept to five to ten families. We have found that fewer than five families will not sufficiently challenge a person to make this ministry a priority and grow in performance. Ten families are not too many for some, whereas we have one lay pastor who has 18 families in her flock. She is able to manage this large number because she is at her ministry nearly every day.

Example. God's call to Timothy through the apostle Paul to "set the believers an example" (1 Tim. 4:12), is also His call to all who would pastor. Of the areas listed in PACE, this is probably the most difficult of all.

Being an example does not suggest that the lay pastor

is the saint, the flock member a sinner; that the one is mature, the other immature; that one is knowledgeable, the other ignorant; that one has arrived, the other still on his way. It does suggest, however, the need to be growing repentant, humble, faithful and unselfish. It suggests we need to be aware of our strengths and weaknesses so as to more firmly root our strengths in Christ and reduce our weaknesses by the power of His Spirit. It also suggests that we are all companions on the same journey, learning from one another just what progress in the Christian walk is all about. Companionship opens into mutual ministry; companions give something of themselves to one another.

Frequent questions that arise are: What if some of my flock members are more mature Christians than I? What if they know the Bible better than I do? Our reply is: Learn from them.

As a professional clergy I have learned much from my people throughout the years. There are lay people who can pray more passionately, have greater wisdom, demonstrate more compassion and know their Bibles better than I. In such cases, I try to be an example of how we can learn from others who are more mature, more gifted. The goal is to be an example, not an expert!

SEVEN COMMITMENTS

Prior to being commissioned, we ask our lay pastors to commit themselves to PACE. Although this is the primary commitment, there are a total of seven:

1. Commitment to PACE
2. Commitment of self to Jesus Christ
3. Commitment of time and energy

4. Commitment of years, to pastor as long as the Lord leads
5. Commitment to continue being equipped
6. Commitment to accountability
7. Commitment to the church and its leadership.

To provide necessary time for understanding and assimilation, and to ask for people's acceptance of each one, it is important in the equipping process to carefully explain these commitments. We do this in the equipping seminar by grouping lay pastors into twos or fours to share their understanding of the commitments with one another and to discuss their readiness to make these commitments. In closing their time together, lay pastors pray for one another.

Once the commitments are made they become the standards by which the lay pastors perform their ministry. Nothing less is acceptable. If the lay pastor or the program begins to accept anything less than these commitments, the importance and the effectiveness of the ministry is lessened and quality and morale start to decline.

Less than acceptable work, procrastination and negative attitudes must be respectfully and gently, but firmly, confronted. If confrontation becomes necessary follow these steps:

First. Review the seven commitments with the lay pastor to clarify the original expectations.
Second. Discover together where the problem is.
Third. Work at the problem and renegotiate if necessary.

67

Some renegotiations we have made include:

1. Reduce the number in the flock to a more manageable number—but no fewer than five.
2. Exchange present flock members for new people.
3. Terminate pastoring temporarily until a personal crisis is over.
4. Release the lay pastors from their commission.

And don't forget to pray together! Prayer is essential to respectful and gentle confrontation.

PASTORING—A WIDE RANGE

The full range of what constitutes pastoring is wide, indeed. At one end it may include discipling, depending on the ability, maturity, training, call and availability of the lay pastor and the readiness of the other person to be discipled. At the other end, depending on the circumstances of need and availability, pastoring may be as simple as thinking caring thoughts about people and letting them know you care.

Two incidents follow which will illustrate these extremes.

One day at lunch one of our husband/wife pastoring teams told me, "We are thinking seriously about resigning. Our flock is resisting our offers to disciple them." They wanted to meet with their flock daily or weekly to work intensively in the Scriptures to bring them to spiritual maturity.

They had brought this type of discipling concept with them from a previous ministering experience. They had a sincere desire to bring their flock to Christian maturity, but their concept muddied their understanding of our definition of pastoring (see p. 39).

The couple was open to learning the difference between discipling people and caring for people pastorally, however. A few days after I explained the difference to them the husband wrote, drawing from his military experience, the following to clarify how they now understood pastoring:

> Imagine a battlefield situation. Two armies oppose each other. Each occupies its own territory, which along some geographical line (a river, valley, road, plain, etc.) meets the other's territory. At that interface, contact occurs. It may only consist of visual observation of the enemy's posts and movements. It may consist of patrols probing the resistance of that interface. Or it may consist of out-and-out battle. It is all contact, a pressure, preferably under one's control, at the interface.
>
> Depending on one's circumstances and objectives, a commander may want to vary the amount of pressure, the length of time engaged and the geographic area covered.

To further clarify the difference I wrote the following in a letter to them:

> Your ministry consists of PACE. The *C* (contact) is not discipling, that is, intensively work-

ing with a person to bring him or her to spiritual maturity. Your contacts are to be pastoral, that is, showing care, concern, acceptance and love. As someone said, "You are love with skin on." The number of contacts and kind (personal visit, mail, telephone, encounter at church, etc.) will vary according to the openness of your people, their need and your availability. As their pastor you will be friendly, encourage them in their church activities and faith, show personal interest, celebrate significant days and anniversaries, inquire as to needs, assure them of your availability and share your faith.

At the other end of the range of pastoring is the experience of Helen Aicholtz learning that often pastoring is just caring and letting the other person know that you do:

Something happened to me last week that has given me a whole new perspective on lay pastoring. My mother, who is 90, has not been corresponding with me of late. She lives in a rest home in Montreal, Quebec, and I was deeply concerned that something was the matter. I called the rest home and they told me there was nothing wrong, that Mother was just having a hard time getting her thoughts together. She was well aware of my letters and my concern and looked forward to hearing from me. They suggested I continue doing what I was doing, *the main thing being that I let her know I cared and was thinking about her.*
It seemed to me that lay pastoring is some-

70

what similar. I believe that I should continue
doing what I am doing, letting my people know I
care.

ACCOUNTABILITY AND APPRECIATION

By requiring monthly reports from our lay pastors, we
have built accountability into our ministry. A member of
our staff, Dr. Gary Sweeten, has said, "It's not what is
expected that gets done, it's what is *inspected.*" The reports
we require keep me in touch with the pastoring activity of
the lay pastors. (And vicariously, these reports keep me in
touch with all the members of our church.)

Appreciation must be shown. People need to know
when they are doing well. They must be affirmed for their
work. How many times we slacken in our commitments or
drop out completely from a project, just because we feel
totally unappreciated. We falsely assume that because we
are Christians we will all continue on tirelessly without
commendation, patiently awaiting our reward in heaven.
Scripture recognizes the human need for affirmation and
calls us to give honor where honor is due (see Rom. 13:7).

SHEPHERDS AND PASTORAL SUPERVISION

The question, "Who pastors the lay pastors?" is inevi-
table and rightly so. Shepherds, who are also lay people
and members of our church, pastor our lay pastors. Shepherds have two roles: (1) to pastor, and (2) to provide pastoral supervision.

As pastors they carry out the same commitments to a
flock of five to ten lay pastors as the lay pastors do to their
flocks—*PACE.* As pastoral supervisors they fill an addi-

71

tional role. They are a support system for the lay pastors in their ministries.

Because lay pastors minister on their own most of the time, they need support and encouragement. They need it from their shepherds and they need it from their flock members. Loneliness and discouragement may set in and lay pastors may actually feel like quitting without the proper pastoral supervision and encouragement.

A typical pastoral supervision question is: Tell me Paul and Sherry, how is your ministry going? A powerful dynamic is released just by asking this question. It causes lay pastors to evaluatively reflect on their pastoring activity in relation to their commitments. In telling how their ministry is going they are being accountable. They are able to spot their own weaknesses readily and in reporting usually tell what those weaknesses are. Not only does this allow for the shepherd to offer suggestions for improvements, but it also opens the door for affirmation, appreciation and encouragement. It makes mutual ministry possible for it is legitimate for the lay pastor to also say, "Now that I've told you how my ministry is going, would you like to tell me how yours is going?"

Part of the supervisory dialogue will focus on a pastoring experience—sort of a case study. Shepherds will want to move through these five steps with their lay pastors:

1. Describe the acts or situations of ministry, perhaps highlighting only one. Example: A woman's husband does not come to church. Her heart is heavy because of this.
2. Identify the central issue needing attention. Example: Spiritual concerns are of little importance to him.

3. Discuss alternative ways of looking at and dealing with the issues. Example: Encourage the wife to be faithful in loving him, to enjoy those things they can do together and to continue growing in her spiritual life.
4. Theologize—attempt to understand what this all means to a Christian. Example: Some people's hearts are hardened (see Heb. 3:8). She can pray for him (see Phil. 4:6). Her life will be a witness to him (see 1 Pet. 3:1-4).
5. Make responsible decisions regarding the act of pastoring. Example: Share her concern and heavy spirit. Covenant to pray faithfully for her and her husband.

The special task of the shepherd is to help the lay pastor tell his or her story. This is not a time to offer packaged answers. This is the lay pastor's hour, not a time for the shepherd to divert the conversation to his own agenda.

TAKE A CLOSER LOOK

To understand the amazing dynamics of pastoral supervision, we need to look more closely at its definition: *Pastoral supervision is a method of doing and reflecting on ministry in which a shepherd and one or more lay pastors covenant together to reflect critically on their ministry as a way of growing in self-awareness, competence, biblical understanding and Christian commitment.*

"Wow! That definition is loaded! Tell me about *doing* and *reflecting* on ministry."

73

1. Critical reflection on acts or situations of ministry (i.e., *doing* ministry) is a way of understanding (a) what took place, (b) why the situations developed as they did and (c) what can be learned from them. The lay pastor is critically reflecting as he or she is telling the act or experience.
2. The person in ministry returns from a supervisory experience into the ministry with new insights and tools. The process flows between action and reflection as indicated in the following diagram:

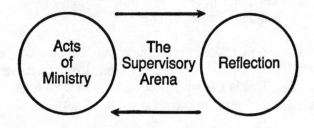

3. What appear to be negative experiences or failures often turn out to be the most useful material from which to learn, even though they may be threatening to the lay pastor to share. Positive experiences call for affirmation and even celebration. Lay pastors who always show their strengths and hide their weaknesses need to be challenged.
4. Supervision is dialogue. The shepherd helps

by (a) listening, (b) making observations and (c) raising questions. Supervision provides a mirror for the lay pastor to reflect on situations in pastoring and see them in all of their dimensions from a new perspective.

"Thank you for explaining that part of your definition. What about those four ways a person will grow by being supervised?"

Self-Awareness—How they are coming across to people. How well they know themselves. How they are feeling about what they are doing.

Competence—Discovering the need for acquiring new skills or improving old ones as they talk about the problems they are running up against. The goal is excellence.

Biblical Understanding—It is imperative that they grow in knowledge of the Bible if they are to grow in effectiveness. As the shepherds share their growth during pastoral supervision, they will be encouraging the lay pastor's growth.

Commitment—To the ministry and to the Lord. Decline, rather than growth, will occur without sharing, nurturing and praying.

Believe me! Lay pastors need support! Interestingly enough, when research was conducted among social workers, it was found that they need this kind of support as well. It was revealed that their satisfaction was dependent upon four things: (1) shared responsibility for cases,

(2) support in difficult cases, (3) help with problems and (4) personal growth. These results give some definite clues to shepherds about their role in support of lay pastors.

Good supervision will be supportive. That is, it will motivate, assure, encourage, strengthen, stimulate, even comfort the lay pastor. It will tap their deeper inner resources, and bring them to the surface for use in this caring ministry.

One of our shepherds, inquiring of a lay pastor who had resigned, asked, "What could I have done better?" The answer he received was: "I would like to have been visited like you wanted me to visit." Shepherds must accept the fact that their pastoring is a model and lay pastors need pastoring too.

Supervision should include lay pastors as full and equal participants in the process. They will respond positively to supervision that treats them as colleagues and will react negatively to supervision that puts them in a subordinate position. It has been discovered that where there is objection to supervision, it is not the supervision itself that is objectionable, but rather its quality that makes the difference.

In other words, a supervisor has to earn the right to supervise. To the degree the lay pastors have been helped to increase their knowledge, improve their skills, be more self-assured and be creative, the supervising shepherd has earned his stripes. The lay pastor is set free rather than bound by supervision.

Supervision should be seen as the kind of intervention into the pastoral activity that strengthens the lay pastors in their ministry and thereby helps them fulfill their call from God to "tend the flock." You may be thinking, "I don't want anybody breathing down my neck." But, when done right, pastoral supervision is pastoral and is a mutually shared joy!

A conscientious shepherd will ask, "What do I have to *be* and *do* to be a good shepherd for my Lord?" In order for a shepherd to fulfill his desire to do a good job of supervising, he must have or work to achieve the following abilities and behaviors:

- Ability to listen
- Recognition and ownership of his own feelings
- Ability to enter into the feelings of other persons (empathy)
- Openness to styles of ministry different from his own
- Ability to create a helping relationship
- Ability to ask the right questions
- Sensitivity to "where the lay pastor is" (Ability to deal with reality as perceived rather than as stated)
- Ability to wait for the lay pastor's growth, to resist the temptation to manage the lay pastor's life
- Recognition of the lay pastor's resistance to growth, ability to know when it is appropriate to probe the resistance and a willingness to do so
- Ability to reflect on the process going on between shepherd and lay pastors so as to produce deeper personal insight
- Ability to share the agenda-setting with the lay pastor.

We have seen in this chapter what lay pastors and shepherds do. Now let us turn our attention to calling people into this ministry.

6

God Calls Them

W hy do you want to be a lay pastor?" We ask people this question on the application form. This sampling of reasons has been copied verbatim from a few of the forms. Reading them will assure a church desiring to start a Lay Pastors Ministry that people will offer themselves for this kind of ministry.

- I enjoy working with people.
- I feel it is the right time to give back a little of the blessing I have received.
- I have always liked helping people and I think this ministry matches many of my gifts.
- Wife: It is an opportunity for me and my husband to be in a ministry together. Husband: To minister together with my wife.
- I desire to utilize counseling training in a Christian ministry.
- To serve the Lord and to enable Christian growth within myself.

- I want to grow in the area of commitment and caring for people.
- I want to be a lay pastor to share my love for the Lord with others.
- I believe the Lord has called me to this.
- I knew I would never make a good ordained minister. This looks like God designed the Lay Pastors Ministry just for me.
- I feel a call. I believe I have a gift for relating to people in a positive way.
- The body of CHPC needs to be strengthened from within. This can only be accomplished effectively by lay pastors who feel the call of the Lord.
- To fulfill God's commandment to serve and minister to others, and to confirm my commitment to Christ.
- We feel there is a need and want to help fulfill the need.
- We believe God has given us a gift and we must use it.
- God has been so good to me that I want to do more for Him. I love people. I love to help.

WHY PEOPLE VOLUNTEER

Marlene Wilson in her book, *How to Mobilize Church Volunteers*,[1] lists eight reasons, shared in interviews and surveys, why people volunteer. My experience with 200 people who have been equipped and commissioned over these eight years is that the reasons she gives for "volunteers" are also true for lay pastors:

1. They want to be needed.
2. They want to help others and make a difference.
3. They want to learn new skills or use skills they already have.
4. They want to belong to a caring community and feel accepted as members.
5. They want self-esteem and affirmation.
6. They want to grow in their faith and share their God-given gifts.
7. They want to keep from being lonely.
8. They want to support causes they believe in.

GOD TAKES THE INITIATIVE

"Moses, Moses! . . . Come, I will send you." God took the initiative in calling Moses by drawing him to the burning bush (see Exod. 3,4). Moses was reluctant. God was persistent. Moses finally gave in. The result was: the people upon whom God had compassion were freed.

God calls people into ministry. The biblical examples are many.

"Samuel! Samuel!" Again God took the initiative (see 1 Sam. 3). Samuel did not recognize at first that it was God who was calling his name. God persisted. Samuel responded. The result was that God revealed His judgment on Eli through Samuel.

"Follow me and I will make you fishers of men (Matt. 4:18-20). Jesus took the initiative with Peter and Andrew. His call was so compelling that they responded immediately. The result was that they became disciples and apostles.

Our conviction from the very inception of this ministry was that God would give a sufficient number of CHPC members pastoral gifts to pastor the entire congregation and that He would also call them into this ministry. Even though at this writing we still do not have a sufficient number of lay pastors to pastor all our people, we are encouraged by a continual flow of new people into the ministry. I believe every church can know that God will do the same within its membership.

NO ARM TWISTING

"Don't say yes until you've thought about it; don't say no until you've prayed about it," is what we regularly tell prospects. Believing that God gifts and calls shapes our approach to people. We do not try to convince people they should be lay pastors. We do not twist arms or lay on guilt. There are always people who will say yes when they are drafted because they do not know how to say no. They do not want to let someone down. They do not want to feel guilty. Our approach is, first, pray a lot. Then we alert people to the possibility that God is calling them. We do not feel the pressure of having to recruit them and they do not feel the pressure of having to say yes. We honestly leave it up to the Lord and them. God calls them. We help them answer. We assure them that a no response is as valid as yes when they have talked with God about it.

For this reason we use the term *calling forth* rather than *enlisting* or *recruiting*. We believe that their call issues from the combined efforts of the Spirit of God, the prospective lay pastor and us. People who come into the ministry motivated by anything less than a call from God either do not last long or are ineffective.

A "CALL"

When our Ministry Group was developing this ministry we faced the question of what constitutes a *call*. We needed an answer if we were to have "called people" do the pastoring. I suggested we needed lay people with a strong sense of a "call from God," like Moses, like Samuel and like I had experienced prior to becoming an ordained clergyman. I felt quite strongly that without this definite "call," people giving themselves to pastoring would either get discouraged and quit, or continue listlessly and not be effective.

As the Ministry Group worked this issue it became clear that *call* might not be the best word to use in seeking people who would be pastors. The members of the Ministry Group felt they and most other people reserved the concept of a "call from God" for those entering the professional ordained ministry. It was obvious that we did not have the same understanding of *call*.

To get some help on settling the issue we surveyed the Pastoral Ministries Committee, a body of 18 committed Christians in our church. We asked two questions without using the word *call*: (1) "Do you believe that what you are doing is what God wants you to be doing?" and (2) "How did you get into the ministry you are doing?" They all believed they were doing what God wanted them to do; however, they gave as many different ways of getting into their ministry as there were people. Some responses were:

1. I was asked by the chairman.
2. The Session appointed me.
3. I felt interested in this.

4. I've always done this kind of work.
5. I was asked to serve and it seemed like any other committee I've been on.

To them, these reasons for being in ministry constituted a "call." We agreed the reality of God's "call" is more evident in reflection than it is at the time of contemplation. It is easier to identify a "call" after we are doing ministry and when someone else helps us identify it as such.

We learned from our study of the book of Ezra that everyone whose spirit God had stirred to go up and rebuild the house of the Lord was "called" (Ezra 1:5). Our conclusion was that however God chose to stir the spirits of people to be lay pastors—psychologically, relationally, organizationally, spiritually, volitionally or emotionally— whatever moved them to make themselves available for pastoring, whatever inner state induced them to respond to our need for lay pastors, we were prepared to understand it as a "call from God" whether they put it in those terms or not.

I must report that in the settling of this issue, and all the others, we prayed a lot, believing the Spirit of God would give us the answers. The success of this ministry has confirmed that the Spirit of God is leading us. However, I must confess that this is seen more easily now than during the time we were experiencing the mix of frustration, struggle and joy of its development.

People's readiness to step forward to offer themselves for ministry cannot be assumed. Their readiness is the fruit of faithful preaching and teaching followed by creating a structure into which people can step. Preaching and teaching the Word about every Christian receiving gifts for ministry created a climate in which people could come

alive to the Spirit. Many were expecting to be in a ministry.

GIFTS FOR PASTORING

Regarding the gifts given by the Spirit, the essential
one for pastoring is *mercy.* Just what is the gift of mercy? It
is the ability to feel genuine empathy and compassion for
people. It is also being able to incarnate Christ's love by
translating these feelings into helpful relationships and
cheerfully done deeds.

I asked a small group of people to write down the gifts
they have to bring to the ministry. Their list does not use
the word but it tells that they have the gift of mercy:

- I am a good listener.
- I am a nurse and am comfortable with visiting
  with people.
- I give people the benefit of the doubt—do not
  jump to conclusions about them.
- I am willing to try anything.
- I am patient.
- My husband died and I understand people in
  grief.

When I tested myself with the Modified Houts Questionnaire[2] I discovered I rated highest in *mercy.* I was glad
to discover this because at that time I had been pastoring
for 35 years without the advantage of a testing instrument.

Some of the other gifts listed in Romans 12:6-8, 1 Corinthians 12:4-11 and 28 and 1 Peter 4:8-11, will be useful
to pastors but *mercy* is sufficient to do effective pastoring.

Dr. Kenneth Kinghorn gives six steps to help Christians discover their gifts.[3]

1. Open yourself to God as a channel for His use.
2. Examine your aspirations for Christ in service in ministry.
3. Identify the needs you believe to be most crucial in the life of the church.
4. Evaluate the results of your efforts to serve and to minister.
5. Follow the guidance of the Holy Spirit as He leads you into obedience to Christ.
6. Remain alert to the responses of other Christians.

Love is an integral part of every gift and precedes or follows every biblical list:

- "Let love be genuine" (Rom. 12:9).
- "If I speak in the tongues of men and of angels, but have not love" (1 Cor. 13:1).
- "Above all hold unfailing your love for one another" (1 Pet. 4:8).

I am not suggesting that every prospective lay pastor be formally tested for gifts, but some may feel the need for testing. They may wish to do a self-test, using Kinghorn's six steps just listed. Even without testing people will be able to understand the gift of mercy and generally will know if they have it.

OUR PLAN

Our plan for alerting people to the need for lay pastors

and that God may be calling them into the ministry includes:

1. Brochures describing the ministry are always available in the literature racks.
2. Articles appear regularly in our monthly church paper.
3. Occasional reference to the ministry and appeals to consider it are made from the pulpit.
4. Ministry Group members are asked to "nurture" individuals to whom the Lord leads them into the ministry.
5. We ask lay pastors to identify those in their flocks who may make good lay pastors and talk with them about the possibility.
6. These activities precede our three annual equipping seminars:
   a. Bulletin announcements giving the purpose, dates and place for the seminar.
   b. Letters mailed to selected, prayed-over people asking them to consider and pray about being lay pastors. This is followed by a phone call from members of the Ministry Group to see if there are questions and to encourage them to register for the seminar.
   c. A registration table is set up three Sunday mornings prior to the seminar, manned by lay pastors and/or Ministry Group members to catch the attention of people who did not receive a letter.
   d. Occasionally our co-pastor, Dr. Ron

Rand, invites a group of people for whom he has been praying to his home to present this ministry to them. Some of our lay pastors are there to tell about what they do and how they feel about pastoring. They also answer questions. The guests are then asked to pray about becoming lay pastors. Two weeks later Ron phones them to ask how they feel the Lord is leading them. Those who feel led register for the seminar.

By praying and doing these things God is giving us a continual flow of people into the ministry. He encourages us by this flow to continue believing that He is giving the pastoral gifts and calling a sufficient number of people into the ministry to pastor every member of our congregation.

CONFIRMING THE "CALL"

Do we accept all who offer themselves? Do we believe that everyone who wants to be a lay pastor is called by God? No to both questions. We have a responsibility under God to assess the personal, spiritual and pastoral qualities of the applicants. The biblical precedents for this are: (1) Moses was to choose those who feared God and who were trustworthy (see Exod. 18:21); (2) the Twelve charged the others to pick out "seven men of good repute, full of the Spirit and of wisdom" to be deacons (Acts 6:3); and (3) Paul gave a long list of qualifications for Titus to use in determining which Christians were to be appointed elders as leaders in the churches in Crete (see Titus 1:5-9).

Our Ministry Group, the people who have ownership

of this ministry, pray for guidance, consider the applicants and confirm their call based on these qualifications:

1. Commitment to Jesus Christ
2. Sound reasons for wanting to pastor (the reasons are spelled out in their application form)
3. Indications of having pastoral gifts
4. Adequately equipped
5. Not overloaded with other ministries or responsibilities.

Occasionally we have to turn people down. When this is necessary we pastorally counsel with them to discover what other ministry they could be in or suggest ways of preparing themselves for a ministry.

We have found that many people are already pastoring—praying for, caring for, feeling responsible for the spiritual and general welfare of specific people—but they have never thought of it as pastoring. So, many people already have experience. It becomes clear when talking with them that the Holy Spirit gave them the gift and they responded to His call long before we structured this ministry and identified them as pastors.

It may be helpful at this point to give the five-step process required to become a lay pastor:

1. Attend an equipping seminar.
2. Fill out an application form.
3. Be accepted (their call confirmed).
4. Be commissioned by the laying on of the hands of elders.
5. Receive a flock to pastor.

Do we have to go through all of this to have lay people pastoring? The commitment made by church officers, such as elders and deacons, is to care for the members of the church. Can't they be the pastors? My response to this question is that *we* have not taken this course. Some of our elders and deacons are lay pastors, not because they are officers, but because they are called by the Lord into this ministry. Some officers are gifted for functions and ministries other than pastoring, such as administration or teaching. Those gifted for pastoring would have their pastoring tied to their time in office.

Our belief is that since people are gifted and called by the Spirit into pastoring their ministry should not cease when the term of office expires. Our lay pastors, whether deacons and elders or not, are commissioned to pastor as long as the Lord leads. Several have been pastoring for as long as we have had the ministry—eight years.

However, I have equipped officers in churches that believed their officers ought to be the lay pastors. Where this is done I would urge two things: (1) Do not press every officer into the pastor mold, for some of them are gifted for other roles; and (2) make provision for those who feel led to continue as pastors after their terms have expired. The Westside Presbyterian Church in Ridgewood, N.J., is doing this. It may be that a smaller church would have to go this route if it is to have its lay people pastoring. Each church needs to assess its own needs, inventory its own people resources, set its own goals for pastoring and design its own structure to reach the goals.

THE PAY-OFFS

There are benefits to pastoring. When I was doing my

Doctor of Ministry Program, the Lay Pastors Ministry being my project, one of the consulting faculty asked, "Mel, what's in it for the lay pastor?" My first reaction was, "What an unchristian question! Who would expect to get anything out of it. This is a ministry of giving, not getting." Biting my tongue I asked, "What do you mean?"

He explained that the lay pastor would need to get something out of it. I gave attention to this new challenge and discovered that there are significant "pay-offs" for the lay pastor, such as:

1. Accelerated spiritual growth. How pleasant that is to a Christian.
2. The joy of new friendships and deep relationships. Being with another in matters of faith bonds two lives as nothing else does.
3. An inner sense of fulfillment that comes from utilizing one's gifts in significant ministry.
4. The caring person is cared for in the act of caring. Jesus said, "He who loses his life for my sake will find it" (Matt. 10:39). As Tom Harris said, "The river of living water flows both directions." Dr. Gary Collins, professor of Psychology at Trinity Divinity School in Deerfield, Illinois, defines this "pay-off" as what he calls the "Helper-Therapy Principle."

> When we help and care for other people, the one who cares is the person who benefits most. There are several reasons for this. When we care for another we often feel the

91

satisfaction and self-esteem that comes from being useful. We are able to observe problems at a distance, and as a result we get a clearer perspective on our own life situations. In reaching out we often feel a greater degree of personal competence and self-worth as a result of making an impact on another person's life. [4]

5. The future benefit—"And when the chief shepherd is manifested you will obtain the unfading crown of glory" (1 Pet. 5:4). This was the promise Peter was privileged to give to people who were to tend the flock of God.

In the next chapter we will discuss how we have been equipping the people who are called to pastor.

Notes:

1. Marlene Wilson, *How to Mobilize Church Volunteers* (Minneapolis, MN: Augsburg Publishing House, 1983), p. 87.
2. *Spiritual Gifts and Church Growth* (Modified Houts Questionnaire) is available from Charles E. Fuller Institute, P.O. Box 989, Pasadena, CA 91102.
3. James L. Garlow, *Partners in Ministry* (Kansas City, MO: Beacon Hill Press, 1981), p. 94.
4. Dr. Gary R. Collins, *The Joy of Caring* (Waco, TX: Word Books, 1980), p. 16.

7

Equipping People to Be Pastors

"You've taught us so well we don't need you anymore," reads the line under a cartoon picturing a group of lay people, probably church officers, making this announcement to their startled pastor. But pastors, this will never happen! You can safely equip your people without any fear of losing your job.

It is imperative that you equip people for the task to which they commit themselves. They want to be equipped and God calls you to do the equipping. Adequate equipping gives people confidence to do what they feel called to do. It maximizes their potential for ministry and informs them that what they are doing is important. An equipped laity is at the heart of the Church renewal we are witnessing in our day.

There are three equippers:

1. Pastors and teachers. "His gifts were that some should be . . . pastors and teachers, to *equip* the saints for the work of ministry" (Eph. 4:11,12).

2. The Holy Spirit. "You shall receive *power* when the Holy Spirit has come upon you" (Acts 1:8). If anything good and lasting is going to happen in lay *or* professional pastoring it will be the Holy Spirit making our efforts and skills effective.
3. The Scriptures. "All scripture is inspired by God and profitable for teaching, for reproof, for correction, and for training in righteousness, that the man of God may be complete, *equipped* for every good work" (2 Tim. 3:16,17). The pastor's life must be formed by the Scriptures and the pastor must grow in the knowledge and skilled use of Scripture so as to grow in effectiveness.

TWELVE UNITS

We give our lay pastors 12 units of equipping in a 15-hour seminar held on a Saturday and Sunday. We offer it three times each year. We have already covered five of the units in the preceding chapters of this book:

Unit 1 The Concept of Lay People Pastoring (chap. 1)
Unit 2 The Biblical Basis (chap. 2)
Unit 3 Who Needs It? (chap. 3)
Unit 4 What a Lay Pastor Does (chap. 5)
Unit 5 Pastoral Supervision (also chap. 5)

These units can be taught in this order by churches who are looking for a manual to use in equipping their people.

UNIT 6—BEING PROFESSIONAL

We need to realize who it is we are equipping. We are equipping nonprofessionals for a task requiring professionalism. I make an important point when I differentiate between being professional and being *a* professional. They are not the same. Being professional means going about one's task in a manner that involves quality performance and quality behavior. A lay pastor can *be* professional in these ways without being *a* professional. We teach in this unit to:

1. Be yourself—Do not imitate anyone, especially a professional clergy. Imitating makes you seem to be someone you are not. Do your pastoring in your own style, your own words and your own personality.
2. Be human—Do not be cold, rigid or impersonal like some professionals tend to be. Genuinely care for people; do not squelch your spontaneous self.
3. Get down to business—Small talk has its place, but you must not neglect getting down to business, getting at what you are there for. Deal with the crisis; give encouragement; ask the questions which will bring problems and joys to the surface; show your faith and your life; pray.
4. Know what you are doing—You will not become a perfect pastor, but you can love and you can use the skills you have acquired thus far. You will be able to learn more and increase your pastoring skills by

taking advantage of additional equipping opportunities.

5. Use your proper authority—Do not disavow the authority given you by the Lord and your church to pastor on their behalf. Your demeanor should build people's confidence in you. Jesus' words in John 15:16 will help you to know you have authority: "You did not choose me, but I chose you and appointed you that you should go and bear fruit."

6. Be dependable—You need to follow through on what you say you are going to do. When you cannot follow through on an appointment, call the people to tell them why you cannot be there or why you will be late.

7. Be available in case of emergency—The classic example of someone being always available in case of emergency is the physician. Because of dedication to the patient he or she is available day or night. Your dedication to your people will make you available to them.

8. Be assertive—You are available but you are not a servant in the sense of responding to every beck and call. If you think you are being manipulated, deal with it by being able to say no and yes appropriately.

9. Know your limitations and make full use of consultations or referrals—It is okay to have limitations. No one has all the answers. When necessary, refer your peo-

pie to those who are professional or who you believe are more competent than you for that particular problem.

10. Be forgiving of yourself—You will make mistakes and you will feel badly about them. You cannot expect to be perfect. Examine the causes for the mistakes, learn from them so as to avoid similar mistakes in the future and then forgive yourself. "To err is human, to forgive is divine" applies to forgiving yourself as well as others.

Since lay pastors are not professionals we can be prepared to accept their less-than-perfect efforts. But as I think back to the many early years of my professional pastoring, lay people had to accept my stumbling efforts. They still do. The longer I am in the ministry as a clergyman the more amazed I am at the tolerance and patience of God's people with their clergy. Accepting less-than-perfect efforts, however, does not include accepting the stumbling incompetence of those not troubling to improve themselves by additional equipping.[1]

UNIT 7—*BEING* PRECEDES *DOING*

We need to be equipping at two levels: *being* and *doing*. Being focuses on what we *are*. Doing focuses on what we *do*.

In our action and achievement-oriented churches it is extremely difficult to believe what we *are* is more important than what we *do*. Because we can give our time and minds to learning what to *do* more easily than we can give our spirits to being what we should *be*, it is difficult to hear what we *are* is more important than what we *do*.

I often conclude my wedding meditations with these words, "Success in marriage is not so much in *finding* the right person as in *being* the right person." How true in marriage! How true in pastoring! Can you believe it? What we *are* is more important than what we *do*.

We who are in ministry need to work on what to *do*, but we need to work harder on what we *are*. I find more and more in my personal life that I am asking God to make me a loving person rather than helping me to love people, to make me a patient person rather than enabling me to show patience, to make me a compassionate person rather than to have compassion, to make me a servant rather than helping me serve people, to make me a generous person rather than helping me give more.

Jesus taught this principle in the Sermon on the Mount, "Every sound tree bears good fruit . . . a sound tree cannot bear evil fruit" (Matt. 7:17,18). If I give adequate attention to growing a sound tree, I will not have to worry about bearing good fruit. I believe God would rather have me be intrinsically loving and caring than have me struggling to perform in ways not true to my nature.

In other words, loving and caring have to be a way of life, not functions of a program we may do at times. God would have it so!

Our Perfect Model

Jesus modeled His teaching. He washed His disciples' feet because He *was* a servant; He was not merely performing a servant's task (see John 13:12-16). He was a loving person; He was not merely loving His disciples on certain occasions (see John 13:34,35). He not only taught that one should lay down his life for his friends (see John

98

15:13), He modeled that teaching in His crucifixion because He *was* a self-giving person. It must be said of Jesus that He did what He did because He was who He was, the Son of God. It must be said of us who pastor that we do what we do because we really are what we are: new creatures in Christ being formed in the likeness of Christ (see Rom. 8:29).

Paul taught this principle. The word *be* appears eight times in 1 Timothy 3:2-13 and is inferred at least another fifteen times. The leader must *be* of certain character before *doing* the work of a leader (bishop or deacon). Our official board took action in accord with this teaching when it restructured itself by stating, "the Session is committed to *becoming* the people of God before *doing* the work of God."

Paul also called Timothy to *be* an example to the believers by being a man of love, a man of faith and a man of purity (see 1 Tim. 4:12). They would know how to talk and how to behave as Christians by observing what Timothy *was*, not only by what he taught. The people who are being pastored will understand and believe what they see more than what they hear. God calls us who pastor to congruence, to bring what we say and what we are into unity.

Peter also taught the principle when he gave the directive to the elders to be examples to the flock (see 1 Pet. 5:3). Their sheep were to be led into Godliness, faithfulness and bearing the fruit of the Spirit. They would be led best by example, by *being* what they were teaching.

One who pastors is to *be* warm, sensitive, understanding and concerned. What Dr. Gary Collins writes in *Christian Counseling* about counselors is also true of pastors: Techniques can only be potent when the counselor has a personality which is inherently helpful—that is, characterized by warmth, sensitivity, understanding, concern and a willingness to confront people in an attitude of love. [2]

Another psychologist reached a similar conclusion, "To be most effective the therapist must be a real, human person . . . offering a genuine human relationship . . . . It is a relationship characterized not so much by what techniques the therapist uses as by what he *is,* not so much by what he does as by the way he does it."[3]

It is clear the professional counselor's effectiveness is tied to what he is as a person. This underscores the requirement that those who pastor must give a lot of attention to what they *are* as Christians as well as to what they *do.*

Another way of talking about the importance of *being* is to use the word *integrity.* Pastoring calls one to be a person of integrity. Just as you know what another person is *really* like, how he or she *really* feels about you; so people who are pastored by others *really* know if they are for real, if they *really* love, *really* care and are *really* committed to them and to Jesus.

Integrity is the transcendent element in pastoral care. [4] Alastair V. Campbell's five definitions of integrity warrant a full discussion on their meaning and implications for pastoring:

1. To possess integrity is to be incapable of compromising that which we believe to be true.
2. To possess integrity is to have a kind of inner strength which prevents us from bending to the influence of what is thought expedient or fashionable or calculated to win praise.

3. It is to be consistent and utterly trustworthy because of a constancy of purpose.
4. Integrity consists in loyalty to an inner truth which cannot be denied whatever the cost.
5. Integrity is an inner steadfastness and an outward honesty and suggests a wholeness upon which such consistency is founded.[5]

There is no way pastoring can be effective without the person doing the pastoring (whether lay or clergy) having integrity. Jesus calls us to integrity by contrasting Gentile authority with serving. Their idea of being great was to "lord it over" people (Matt. 20:25). But Jesus' idea was: "Whoever would be great among you must be your servant" (v. 26). Two of the disciples thought the key principle to greatness was a high position of power. Jesus' admonition and instruction to them helps us who pastor to believe fulfillment of our call is neither in designated role (ordination or commission) nor in knowledge, but in being a person of integrity.

Integrity—in other words the genuineness of our faith, the authenticity of our care and the congruence between our internal and external—makes a pastoring relationship possible. And *it is the relationship that makes the pastoring effective.* The fact that our lay pastors have a strong desire to be effective in pastoring underscores the need for integrity, for without integrity they will not be effective. If they are not effective, they will not see much happen. From here on the spiral is downward. If they do not see things happening, they will get discouraged, quit or hang on only out of loyalty.

A good relationship is the key to being an effective pastor. What is the key to a good relationship? Integrity!

Equipping people with skills (how to *do*) without equipping them with integrity (how to *be*) is to equip them for ineffective, inadequate, unauthentic pastoring and will only delude them. You will set them up for failure. Even in secular counseling, the prominent therapist Carl Rogers tells it was gradually driven home to him that he could not be of help by means of any intellectual or training procedure. No approach which relies upon knowledge, upon training, upon acceptance of something which is taught, is of any use. His experience forced him to recognize that change comes about in a relationship.[6] What Rogers means by *change* in counseling is to be understood as *effectiveness* in pastoring.

UNIT 8—IMPERATIVES FOR PERSONAL SPIRITUAL HEALTH

Since *being* is so important, we must always be working at it. We teach two imperatives which, if acted upon, will produce a spiritually healthy person.

Spending time daily with God is imperative number one. He calls us to be like Him! (See Eph. 5:1.) Think of it—to be like Him! And the only way pastors can be like Him is to spend time with Him. Since we tend to take on the character and personality of those with whom we are close, the journey inward *with* God is a prerequisite to the journey outward *for* God!

"God, make me like you!" I heard that prayer come from my lips one morning as I was on the journey inward.

I usually spend an hour with God between 6:30 and 7:30 A.M. each day.[7] One morning I was reading and meditating on Psalm 103:8, "The Lord is merciful and gracious, slow to anger and abounding in steadfast love." In thinking deeply about the character of God as sketched in this verse—merciful, gracious, patient, loving—and being struck by the considerable difference between me and God, I found myself asking God to make me like Him. If every pastor, lay and clergy, could be more like God in mercy, grace, patience and love, the pastoring would be more nearly what God wants it to be. One of the most important units of equipping is to give people the tools for getting together daily with God and solicit their commitment to do it.

When spending time with God, read Scripture and pray. As to the first, Richard Foster reminds us that the central purpose of reading or studying the Bible is neither to achieve doctrinal purity nor to amass information, but to effect "inner transformation."[8] We do well to follow seriously his four steps:

1. Repetition
2. Concentration
3. Comprehension
4. Reflection[9]

As to the second, I find it a great help to write out a prayer list. This is the simple technique of making a "shopping list" of requests. One request on that list may be "God, make me like you—*merciful* to people who wrong me, *gracious* in showing favor to everyone rather than just a select few, *patient* with people who irritate me and *loving* throughout the day."

We need to be specific in our praying. Rather than "Lord, help me be patient today;" it is, "Lord, help me be patient with my neighbor when his dog is barking tonight and I have to confront him about it." In our equipping seminars we teach the new lay pastors to pray specifically by asking them to take three minutes to write down five specific personal prayer requests. Then they are given two minutes to silently pray about them.

We can use our imaginations to visualize our praying. One picture is worth a thousand words whether visualized in the mind or drawn on paper. We teach visualization. Visualization is thinking in pictures what the answered prayer would look like.

For example, I asked a man to use his imagination as he prayed to see himself greeting his alienated daughter as she came home from work with these words: "Michelle, we haven't talked for a long time. How about us sitting down with some coffee and trying to talk for a few minutes." He was excited by the specificity as he began to use his imagination while praying. I believe the Holy Spirit will guide the imagination, enabling us to be specific in our praying.

Being persistent in prayer is urged by our Lord in the parable of the unjust judge who gave in to the widow because she kept coming to him. "Because this widow bothers me, I will vindicate her" (see Luke 18:1-7). By delaying his response, I think God sometimes helps us discover how much we really want or need what we are asking for.

"When I am not praying as I should, I am not pastoring as I should," Dr. Jerry Kirk told our lay pastors on one occasion. I truly believe that most of the ineffectiveness, most of the failures, most of the discouragements and most of the problems in pastoring will be taken care of by the acceptance and practice of this imperative.

It is a challenge to every pastoring person to ponder these words of Richard Foster, "It is the discipline of prayer itself that brings us into the deepest and highest work of the human spirit . . . to pray is to change. Prayer is the central avenue God uses to transform us."[10] We dare not assume our lay pastors will practice this first imperative of spending time daily with God without being equipped to do it. Most Christians of any maturity at all know how to do this but I find that many are not doing it. I also find that I need to be called back to it more frequently than I want to admit.

I tell the story of my 10-year-old granddaughter in Duluth, Minnesota. She brought me a cup of hot chocolate a few minutes after we stopped to spend a day with her and her family. It was one of these cups with printing on the outside. It read, "Kiss Me. I'm Cute." As she stood a few feet from me, I turned the cup so she could read the words. Silence. No action.

Finally, I said, pointing to the words, "Tracey, do you see this?"

"Yes, I read it." She was nodding her head in her inimitable way.

Then, looking deeply into her brown eyes, I said, "I know you read it. I want you to *do* it." Concerning our spending time with Him, God may have to address us with those same words.

Being filled with the Holy Spirit is imperative number *two*. Both the human and the divine participate in pastoring. You are the human. The Holy Spirit is the divine. He is *with* and *in* the believer (see John 14:16,17). The pastor, to be authentic and effective in tending part of God's flock, is to be filled with His Spirit who is already in him (see Rom. 8:9-11; Eph. 5:18).

"Without God we cannot; without us God will not," Augustine taught.

105

A gardener's pastor was visiting him. The pastor, awe-struck by the beauty of the garden, said, "What a scene of beauty God has created!" Respectfully but firmly the gardener replied, "You should have seen what it was like when God had it by Himself." If pastoring is to happen, God and you will be working together at it; loving, caring, praying, nurturing, helping, visiting, confronting and listening.

"As the Father sent me, so I send you." When Jesus left the world He committed His cause to His disciples. On the Day of Pentecost He gave His Spirit to enlighten and empower them for His cause. I understand the Spirit of Jesus is at the same time the Spirit of the Father. And in some way, incomprehensible to our human minds, their Spirit eternally proceeds from them (see John 15:26). This assures us that the same Spirit who enlivened the first disciples has entered us modern disciples to enliven us as well.

To add to our understanding of the Holy Spirit so as to rely on Him for effective pastoring, we need to know how Paul's and Luke's writings about the Spirit differ but also complement each other. For Paul it is a once-and-for-all action of the Spirit at conversion that incorporates us into the Body of Christ, enables inner growth and equips for ministry (see Rom. 8:9-11; 1 Cor. 12:4-11). For Luke it is the continuing action of the Spirit by which God gives us power for effective witness and ministry (see Luke 24:48,49; Acts 1:8). The former is inward. The latter is outward. Whether inward or outward, the power of the Spirit is the power of pastoring.

"Be filled with the Spirit" is the directive in Ephesians 5:18. Knowing the theology of the Spirit will not fill a pastor with the Spirit. Whereas receiving the Spirit is passive and happens when we receive Christ whether we know anything about the Spirit or not, being *filled* with the Spirit is active. You must be intentional about it. I asked an introvert—a shy young man one time how he could bring back such glowing reports of his visits. His reply was, "I just ask the Holy Spirit to fill me and then I knock on the door." That is being intentional.

A suitable prayer for a pastor who is about to make a contact, whether via phone, letter or visit, is, "Holy Spirit, fill me this moment for pastoring. I need a love, wisdom and power beyond my love, wisdom and power. Fill me, Lord. Thank you. Amen."

At this point in our equipping seminars we get into pairs to share with each other the Campus Crusade booklet, *How to Be Filled with the Holy Spirit.* [11] Our time together is concluded by praying for the Holy Spirit to fill us. It is one of the most meaningful moments of the equipping experience.

We turn now from equipping to *be* to equipping to *do.* Remembering the heart of pastoring is PACE, we are ready for the next unit.

UNIT 9—THE ANATOMY OF A VISIT

We ask our lay pastors to make their First Visit within 30 days of their commissioning. The day following the laying on of hands we mail a letter to each member of their flock informing them that they now have a lay pastor. We tell them who it is. This letter goes out over my signature with the assurance that they can look forward to the First Visit and a good relationship.

The visit is to include these components:

1. Prayer prior to the phone call to set the time for the visit.
2. Prayer prior to making the visit.
3. Identification—At the door give your name and state your purpose for being there.
4. Small talk—this can be about pictures, plants, pets, weather, job, etc.
5. Inquiry about family, community, church, etc. This kind of friendly conversation begins to build the relationship.
6. Sharing common interests and concerns, church news, faith.
7. Explanation of the Lay Pastors Ministry—making sure they understand PACE. Clarifying expectations. Letting them know you are available for prayer or other needs and giving them a folder that explains the ministry.
8. Prayer before leaving.
9. Departure—leave graciously. Do not overstay. Express your gratitude to them for receiving you. State your expectations for another contact.
10. Alertness and sensitivity—to their interests, needs, family situation, spiritual state.
11. Logging the visit—This enables you to connect your visits so as to build a relationship and build the flock member's faith. Names of children and pets should be recorded. Significant events such as anniversaries and birthdays should be

logged. Place of employment and school will be helpful data for the future. A record of hobbies and interests will be helpful. The best time and place for the next visit should be noted.

12. Make out the First Visit Report and submit it.[12]

"Hello, this is David Shaw, your new lay pastor. I am calling to suggest an evening to visit you and get acquainted." David is simulating a phone call to make an appointment for the First Visit.

We discovered the need to role-play the entire First Visit, from the phone call through filling out the report. It is done by dividing the seminar group in twos. Each takes a turn practicing the visit. This role-playing has become an enjoyable part of the seminar and has proven to be a valuable experience when it comes time to make that real First Visit.

The First Visit has a special significance that is different from subsequent visits; it prepares the way for the total pastoring relationship. Having been in the home enables subsequent contacts by cards or letters, telephone or informal encounters at the grocery store or church, to have a depth they would not have without that First Visit.

It takes a long time to learn some things. After five years into the ministry, we made an addition to the preparation for the First Visit. Now we ask experienced lay pastors to take the new lay pastors with them on one of their regular visits. This is done before the new lay pastors make their First Visits. This practice has been very helpful to the inexperienced people and is also enjoyed by the experienced lay pastors.

To read the following report on the First Visits made by Nellie Pratt is to look into her spirit. It is the beginning of her life touching the lives of others on behalf of Jesus Christ and His Church. (This report is unedited.)

1. A pleasant visit. I had called in June just after her husband had come home after having heart surgery. She had recently suffered a broken hand. He wasn't ready for them to have visitors. He is much better now and her hand is improving. I had written and sent my card so she had my telephone number. We were both glad to meet and had a good conversation.

2. A most enjoyable visit. Miss Jones had intended to take the Lay Pastor Seminar but became ill and could not. She is involved in establishing a Christian support group in a hospital where she is a physician in residency. Prayers will be for success in this undertaking.

3. I felt that we both enjoyed the visit. She had not had a lay pastor before. She invited me to stop at her office anytime. I will call and visit. I'm concerned because she has dropped some church activities. I will pray concerning this.

4. We had a pleasant time together. She is so appreciative about having a lay pastor, has had Mr. Koch before. She is a very busy lit-

tle person and enjoying good health right now. I have known Mary in Tuesday Evening Circle for many years. She is an inspiration to me. I will call and visit frequently and pray for her health and happiness.

5. I have been unable to visit this lady. First call (telephone) she was very hostile—said she was looking around for a new church. She took my number (I think) and said she'd call when she could see me, but never did. I called again but she still would not make an appointment. On July 10, I called and she was on her way to Hamilton to take an aunt to a hospital. After the aunt is placed (she has phlebitis) Mrs. Wilson and daughter are going to Myrtle Beach for two weeks, then we will get together. She actually sounded friendly and called me by my first name. If this doesn't work out I will go anyway and leave the booklet and card on her door if she is not home.

6. I have talked with them three times. They are very agreeable but we haven't been able to get together. Mr. Robinson is in Seattle and his wife is leaving July 11 to join him. They will be back in town around July 22, and we plan to meet shortly after.

7. I went at the time (7:30 P.M.) that we had arranged but found no one at home. I left the booklet and my card after waiting a reasonable time. Mrs. Smith called about 9:00 P.M. She had been delayed in getting home. We will make another appointment.

UNIT 10—AUTHORITY TO PASTOR

If lay people are to be authentic pastors they must be given the authority to pastor. I briefly stated in Unit 6 (page 96) on "Professionalism," that lay pastors are to use their proper authority and not denounce it. That brief statement needs to be expanded.

Your role of lay pastor is a designated role to which you are called and commissioned. I understand from Hebrews 13:7,17 that your flock members are to "remember," "obey" and "submit" to you. I also understand from the same Scripture that God calls you to watch over their souls as men and women who will give account. I further understand that they are to imitate your faith. That is authority!

Both your Lord and your church give you authority. They have not given you these awesome pastoral responsibilities without also giving you the necessary authority to carry them out.

First of all, Jesus has given you authority: "I chose you and appointed you" (John 15:16). The *King James Version* uses a stronger word for *appointed—ordained*. In addition to choosing you, He has given you the keys to the kingdom (see Matt. 16:19). In his commentary, *Notes on the New Testament,* Albert Barnes explains that he who has the key has the power of access to, and the general care of the house. The key is a symbol of superintendence, an indication of power and authority. Think of it! Your Lord Jesus Christ has given you authority to pastor.

Second, your church has given you authority. It is inconceivable that your church would withhold that which your Lord has already given. Your church gives you authority by the action of the official board designating, equipping and commissioning lay people as pastors of the members of the church. The elders who laid hands on you as you were commissioned passed it on to you. They charged you with the sacred responsibility to care for your flock.

Two questions need to be answered. First, what is the nature of this authority?

1. It is serving, not commanding (see Mark 9:33-35).
2. It is being respectful, not looking down on (see Rom. 12:3).
3. It is being exemplary, not domineering (see 1 Pet. 5:3).
4. It is being equal, not superior (see Rom. 12:10).
5. It is being mutually submissive, not coercive (see Eph. 5:21).

Rather than a humble, serving spirit causing you to belittle the special gifts you have for your special role, it enables you to release these gifts in power! It will earn for you the right to pastor—to "be with," to hold accountable, guide, admonish, confront, affirm, encourage, strengthen, nurture, love and be respected.

Please note that the right to pastor has to be *earned*. Even though the authority was given to you by your Lord and your church, you must use it properly and in the right spirit. We hear of people who "lord it over" others. It is clear that a Christlike spirit does just the opposite.

The second question: What does it mean to have authority?

It means to have the spirit we just talked about. Your

authority puts you in a position to truly serve. It creates a relationship in which you can give yourself to a greater extent than if you were not given the pastoring role. Can you hear Jesus saying, "If you aspire to be a good pastor, be a servant"? (Author's paraphrase of Mark 9:35.)

To have authority also means to be accountable to those who placed you in this position—your Lord and your church. As a lay pastor you are not to abdicate this authority. You are to use it, knowing you will have to give an account of how you have used it. How good it is to be affirmed by those who have laid hands on you and those who pastor you. How good it will be to hear in that coming day after you have given the final account, "Well done, good and faithful servant" (Matt. 25:23).

Finally, to have authority means to be *authoritative* without being *authoritarian*. The difference between these two depends on the locus of power. What C. Peter Wagner writes about a professional pastor is also true for lay pastors:

> When the pastor realizes he is an under-shepherd, receiving his authority from the Word of God, he gives *authoritative* leadership . . . .
> When the pastor localizes power in his personality, he gives *authoritarian* leadership. [13]

The difference is between *lordship* and *leadership*. Only Jesus is Lord! You and I are servants.

UNIT 11—THE LAY PASTOR LISTENS

A wise old owl
Lived in an oak,

114

The more he saw
The less he spoke;
The less he spoke,
The more he heard;
Why can't we be
Like that wise bird?

—Author unknown

The skill of listening is one we know God would call us to develop. We need to learn as early as possible to talk less and listen more. James 1:19 counsels us to be "quick to hear, slow to speak." If we truly love people and want to show we care, we need to listen for the feelings and conditions behind the words.

There is the story of a young man who visited his Rabbi and became so overwhelmed by the emotional experience that he cried out, "Rabbi, I love you dearly." The Rabbi, who was both touched and amused by his student's devotion, asked, "Tell me, my son, you say that you love me, but where do I hurt? What ails me?" The perplexed young man responded, "I do not know where you hurt, Rabbi, but nevertheless I love you dearly." To this the Rabbi replied, "But how can you say you love me when you do not even know where I hurt and what brings me pain?"[14]

For the young man to learn of the Rabbi's hurts would require that he listen to the feelings and to what is *not* being said as well as to what is being said. The point is well made of the relationship between love and knowing another's pain.

Since time in our seminars does not permit full training in listening skills, we give only a few elementary principles. Because it is such a complex skill and of such impor-

115

tance, we recommend as strongly as possible that lay pastors take additional training in listening as soon as they can. Here are the basics we teach:

1. While we are listening we can be giving ourselves to understand what we are hearing. We can listen for feelings and for what is *not* being said as well as to what is being spoken.
2. While we are listening we can be learning. To help us learn we can be asking ourselves, "Why is this person telling me this, and why is he or she telling me now?"
3. While we are listening we can be thinking. We can listen to 500 or 600 words per minute, while we can speak only 150 words per minute, so there is what is called "lag time" for thinking.
4. By listening we are encouraging other people to talk about what they need or want to talk about, showing that we are interested in them and what they have to say. We are able to be sure we are understanding what they are intending to say.
5. People have a deep need to be heard. They may have no one who will hear the symphony of their verbals, nonverbals and feelings with empathy, understanding and genuineness other than their lay pastors.

Ways to Listen

There are two primary ways to listen. The first is *pas-*

sive. This means that you must be present and interested. Give a smile, a friendly nod, a gesture of concern that tells the person you are with him.

In passive listening we do not simply listen in order to know what to say. If that were so, then speaking would be more important than listening. But it is not! Listening is more important because people's inner struggles, doubts, fears, joys, excitements and gratitudes need to be heard; but they cannot be heard unless someone is listening.

It is as simple as that! People feel affirmed when they know they are heard. Giving your whole attention to another is in itself a gracious act.

The second way of listening is *active*. Active listening assures both you and the person talking that you are understanding.

What I read somewhere and memorized makes the point so clear, "I know you believe you understand what you think I said, but I am not sure you realize that what you heard is not what I meant." How we need to be sure we have heard what the other person is intending to say.

Rather than an advice-giving or question-answering response, active listening is trying to accurately reflect what you think the other person is intending to say. This is sometimes called reflective listening or paraphrasing. If it is a problem the person is talking about, this listening skill is so effective that the solution may dawn on the person while talking. This may happen without even a suggestion from the listener.

Such are the dynamics of active listening. The speaker will have the satisfaction of discovery! The solution is often within the individual. Active listening merely brings it to the surface.

An active listening dialogue might go like this:

Flock Member:	I just don't know how to handle this problem with our pastor.
Lay Pastor:	He is doing something that you question.
Flock Member:	I don't really have a right to question what he does but he doesn't ask me to go visiting with him anymore.
Lay Pastor:	You used to make home visits with him.
Flock Member:	I surely did. Quite regularly. Every week or two. I even accompanied him on taking communion to the sick.
Lay Pastor:	You enjoyed that.
Flock Member:	It made me feel I was doing something worthwhile.
Lay Pastor:	You feel that he doesn't want you to go with him now.
Flock Member:	I'm not sure that he doesn't *want* me to go with him. I have thought that he felt I was not good enough, but how would I know for sure?
Lay Pastor:	You would like to know for certain why he is not asking you.
Flock Member:	I surely would. Do you suppose I could just come out and ask him?

Lay Pastor:	You are thinking that you could approach him with the question.
Flock Member:	You know, I believe I could do that. I'll call him tomorrow morning and ask to see him.

UNIT 12—CONFIDENTIALITY

"I can't believe I told you all of this," Lee confessed.

"You can trust me with it," Mark promised. "I will keep it confidential."

To say that confidentiality is vitally important is not an exaggeration. Confidentiality is part of our responsibility as pastors and is one of the foundations of a good *helping* relationship. Upon this foundation is built trust, honest communication and freedom for the person to express personal thoughts, feelings and release. When people you are pastoring view you as a person in whom they can confide, they are extending to you a special gift of trust. You must handle such a special gift respectfully and responsibly. To break the confidentiality of a pastoral relationship is a sure way to lose this special gift of trust. If the flock member no longer believes you can be trusted to keep to yourself what is shared in private, your helping relationship with that person will be seriously crippled. Once this person's trust is lost, you may discover that you do not have an opportunity to regain it.

Furthermore, breaking confidentiality with a person may have the added effect of encouraging a particular person to believe that he or she cannot trust anyone with private feelings and problems. During the course of pastoring, people will share with you some very private things about their life situations and about themselves. If such information were somehow to become public knowledge, in all probability the people would become embarrassed, ashamed or deeply hurt. And in some situations the reputation of those people might even be damaged.

Just as we show love to people by the personal care we give, we also need to demonstrate this love by not saying anything to others that might damage their well-being. You see, confidentiality is a serious matter. Because of this, we need to carefully consider two things: *What* is confidential in a pastoral relationship, and *how* can we make sure that it remains confidential?

The difference between public and private knowledge must be respected. Public knowledge is that which is known by other people or could be made known without running the risk of sharing something the person wants kept confidential. Knowledge such as the birth of a child, an extended convalescence, a death or an accident is public knowledge.

Private knowledge is that which other people do not know or at least should not know. Such situations could be an unwanted pregnancy, family conflict, psychiatric hospitalization, some kinds of surgery or other physical conditions, some aspects of divorce and drug abuse problems or alcoholism.

Often there will be *gray* areas in pastoral conversation about which the pastor will have to make a judgment as to whether its knowledge is public or private. He may want to pass on information so that concerned people can pray or express their sympathy and concern, or offer help. When there is doubt certain information concerning a person is public or private the rule is: Always check with the person and get permission before it is shared. An example of the *gray* area is a person who is hospitalized with cancer and may or may not want this to become public knowledge. Since some would want to make it known and others would not, it is imperative to get the person's permission before sharing it.

Sometimes, even though you do have permission to share a situation with others, it may not be wise to do so. The person giving the permission may not realize the information would be hurtful to him or her, or members of the family, neighbors and others. In the area of confidentiality it is helpful to know the difference between gossip and slander. According to one definition, gossip is telling an untruth; slander is telling the truth for the purpose of hurting another. Sharing some kinds of information even though given permission, may unintentionally border on slander.

Confidentiality requires the lay pastor to deny requests for information from concerned or prying people. Sometimes we are tempted to break confidentiality because we believe the information might help the person. It takes both self-discipline and assertiveness to maintain the principle of confidentiality.[15]

CONTINUE TO BE EQUIPPED

Whether on the topic of confidentiality or any other topic, people doing pastoring will need to commit themselves to continue being equipped. We made one serious mistake in putting this ministry together. We failed to plan for our lay pastors to continue being equipped after being commissioned.

Two years ago we took steps to correct this oversight

by challenging our lay pastors to Second and Third Levels of equipping.

- Level One—the 15 hours of basic equipping.
- Level Two—courses in listening, interpersonal skills and Bible.
- Level Three—seminars in counseling and evangelism. Also, more Bible.

Another way we are correcting this oversight is to periodically purchase a selected book for each of our lay pastors. Then we call them together in small groups for a two-hour introductory study. They take it from there. Two excellent books we have given our lay pastors are *The Joy of Caring* by Gary Collins and *Standing By* by Juanita Ryan.

Most professional pastors take continuing education courses annually. Many churches, realizing the importance of this, provide funds for their clergy to grow in this way. This priority on maximizing gifts, time and energy provides a model for lay pastors to continue growing in pastoring skills.

Time for Questions

Questions are an important part of the equipping experience. Time will have to be provided for questions and answers in the schedule. These are the kinds of questions that can be expected:

- Can we select the number of families we will pastor?
- Can we decide to become lay pastors at a later time?

- Will there be some place lay pastors can go for help and further training?
- How do we get our flock?
- What are the specific support mechanisms?
- If a lay pastor receives too heavy a load of people who need extensive ministry, can the load be adjusted?
- Are the flocks assigned in a geographical area?
- Do husband and wife have a flock jointly or separately?
- When both husband and wife are lay pastors and they have family responsibilities, is it acceptable for one to carry the major responsibility for visiting and the other make contacts?
- Can we start with fewer than five families to pastor?
- Can you give us an idea of typical occurrences during an average month?
- What about the length of time to this commitment?
- Can we take on new or more people to pastor if we see the need?
- Will there be training for lay pastors in special fields such as the chronically ill, terminally ill, marital problems and others?
- Shouldn't singles minister only to other singles, men minister to men and women to women?
- How do we deal with spiritual questions?
- How do we deal with financial needs?

- Are there funds available for cards, gifts and other expenses?
- In the process of implementing this ministry, some will not have lay pastors. How will they feel?
- How much time each month is required for pastoring?

The equipper should answer the questions he can, defer some to those who can answer, not hesitate to take them under advisement, not hesitate to state that some answers can only be found in the process of doing the ministry or simply say, "I don't know the answer to that question."

Motivation

"I need to talk with you sometime about my pastoring. I don't seem as excited about it as I used to be. It may be I need something that is a little more active." I heard what Frank was saying. After three years of good pastoring he was losing his enthusiasm, vision and sense of call.

Motivation is a part of equipping but continues beyond the basic equipping as a perpetual need. Two kinds of motivation are needed: (1) that which *brings* a person into the ministry, and (2) that which *keeps* a person in the ministry.

That which motivates a person to go into a ministry will not necessarily motivate the person to continue. In fact, idealism may move a person into the ministry. The realism of doing the ministry may cause one to lose interest unless new motivational dynamics are provided.

By motivation we mean: that which incites a person to action from within. Something deep within the lay pastor must come alive in order to pastor and be kept alive if the pastoring is to be fulfilling to him or her and helpful to those being pastored.

Dr. Frederick Herzberg has identified what he believes are motivational factors: (1) a sense of achievement, (2) recognition for work done, (3) a feeling of importance and interest in the work itself, (4) an opportunity to take responsibility and (5) an experience of growth and development.[16] When these factors are experienced by the lay pastors their needs are being fulfilled and they are, therefore, inwardly motivated. It becomes the responsibility of the shepherds and clergy to facilitate these motivational factors.

Some of our efforts to motivate are:

1. A quarterly meeting of the lay pastors.
2. A response to each monthly report either by mail or phone.
3. Regular contacts by the shepherds.
4. Pictures and articles in every issue of our church paper.
5. A monthly newsletter to our lay pastors which we appropriately named "The Shepherds' Call."
6. Occasional phone calls, letters, individual conferences or chance contacts at church by me or my assistant.
7. Our Ministry Group praying for each lay pastor and informing them of our praying.
8. An annual ministry celebration and recognition banquet.

No matter how thorough the equipping or the depth of

commitment, those who do the ministry will have to struggle with problems. Rather than a liability, however, problems create learning opportunities and help to mature lay pastors. So, let us move from equipping lay people for pastoring to helping them manage those problems that may arise.

Notes:

1. The thoughts presented in this unit are based on concepts contained and more fully developed in one training module of the Stephen Series Leaders Manual bearing the title "Being Professional," © 1983 by Stephen Ministries. Adaptation and use is by permission of Stephen Ministries, 1325 Boland, St. Louis, MO 63117.
2. Dr. Gary R. Collins, *Christian Counseling* (Waco, TX: Word Books, 1980), pp. 14, 15.
3. Ibid.
4. Alastair V. Campbell, *Rediscovering Pastoral Care* (Philadelphia, PA: Westminster Press, 1981), p. 23.
5. Ibid., pp. 23-25.
6. Campbell, *Rediscovering Pastoral Care*, p. 21.
7. The account is given in a small folder titled "Getting Together with God," free for writing to the author of this book, College Hill Presbyterian Church, 5742 Hamilton Ave., Cincinnati, OH 45224.
8. Richard Foster, *Celebration of Discipline* (New York: Harper & Row, 1978), pp. 59, 60.
9. Ibid., pp. 30-40.
10. Ibid., p. 39.
11. Available from Campus Crusade for Christ International, Arrowhead Springs, San Bernardino, CA 92414.
12. A video tape of a First Visit is available from CHPC, Lay Pastors Ministry, 5742 Hamilton Ave., Cincinnati, OH 45224. Phone (513) 541-5676.
13. Peter C. Wagner, *Leading Your Church to Growth* (Ventura, CA: Regal Books, 1984), p. 115.
14. Quote from Rabbi Yechiel Eckstein in November 1984, *Christian Life* article "What Christians Need to Know About Jews."
15. Much of this unit is adapted from The Stephen Series and used by permission from the Stephen Ministries, 1325 Boland, St. Louis, MO 63117.
16. Quoted by D.B. Heusser, *Helping Church Workers Succeed* (Valley Forge, PA: Judson Press, 1980), p. 32.

8

Managing the Difficulties

Beginning a ministry is like beginning a marriage. There is a honeymoon period. These notes were made early in our Lay Pastors Ministry history:

> The first fruits of implementation were evident at the first report meeting. Nearly all lay pastors had visited every family in their flocks. Their spirits had been ignited by these first experiences of pastoring and they had been graciously received in all but one home. [1]

The honeymoon phase was followed by the reality of having to work at it. Difficulties emerged and had to be managed. Both we who lead the ministry and those doing it have found that the problems have been challenging. They have matured us and have tested both the viability and validity of the lay pastors ministry. We are pleased to report the ministry has not only survived the problems but has become stronger because of having to deal with them.

COMMON DIFFICULTIES

Through our years of working with the ministry, we have encountered at least seven standard difficulties. To know how we are managing them may be of help to other churches who are past the honeymoon phase. For those of you who are not yet "married"—only courting the ministry at this point—awareness of potential problems may help forestall some and prepare you to manage others.

Difficulty Number One: Some People Think They Do Not Need a Lay Pastor

They probably do not understand the purpose of a lay pastor so they have no way of knowing what they think they do not need. Nellie Pratt met this kind of resistance and wrote the following in her First Visit Report:

> Mr. Dean was not at home. Mrs. Dean had told me on the phone that she didn't want this "involvement," but I explained exactly what we were pledged to do. She then consented for me to visit. She was a little cool at first but soon opened up and I was amazed at her need for someone to listen. She didn't stop talking until a daughter called her to come pick her up. I left almost immediately. She took my hand and thanked me and said it was wonderful to know someone cared for them.

This lay pastor met resistance with a positive offer. The offer was accepted and a long pastoring relationship followed.

Everybody needs to be pastored! Hear that? Everybody! Not only those requesting it or those who are open to receiving it. It is very important that every lay pastor believes this. When they have accepted this fact they will be able to speak convincingly and with integrity to people who are reluctant to receive them. Lay pastors, themselves, are being pastored by a lay pastor called a Shepherd. Telling the resisters this may help to get them past their resistance. The fact that the Session has officially adopted the Lay Pastors Ministry as the way the church will do its pastoring helps those who are to be pastored to accept the ministry.

Less pastoring. When flock members persist in not accepting lay pastors, the lay pastors may have to drop to a reduced level of pastoring. They may be limited to praying faithfully and sending Easter, Christmas and birthday cards. They may have to be content with knowing that God would have them love, care for and pray for the resisting persons until their acceptance of personal contacts. Great patience is required. The formula we use for such situations is *MP/MC* (maximum prayer/minimum contact).

We very rarely release a resister from the lay pastor's flock. That person probably does not want to see some other lay pastor either. God would have *every* member cared for and prayed for by someone, even if it must be from a distance. Lay pastors need help to see that this reduced level *is* pastoring. It is all the pastoring that can be done at this time. Reducing the number of attempted personal contacts is actually the loving and pastoral thing to do because it demonstrates respect for the person's right of privacy. MP/MC has a positive effect on the development of the pastoring relationship for the future, especially when the person encounters a crisis.

This seemingly dormant period of time tests the commitment of the lay pastor. To continue praying when there is no visible change in the resistance stretches our belief in the ministry of intercessory prayer. I feel good about being able to report that we have found very few resisters hold out forever.

Difficulty Number Two: Some People Are Very Busy and Therefore Difficult to Contact or Visit

First, it must be realized that some people are extremely busy. Their schedules seem to them too full to permit another activity such as a home visit. This calls for patience and persistence with sensitivity. The lay pastor may be able to make brief phone calls only and send letters and cards until the schedule opens up. A balance between respect for people's time and the call of God to "tend the flock" needs to be struck. Admittedly, it is not easy for an activistic-oriented lay pastor to be content with doing little things. Patience and faithfulness may have to be learned in order to do big things later on. It is sort of like the principle of delayed gratification. It will help to know Jesus will say, "Well done, good and faithful servant; you have been faithful over a *little,* I will set you over much" (Matt. 25:21).

Difficulty Number Three: Lay Pastors Get Busy and Neglect Their Flocks

As Pogo said, "We have met the enemy and it is us." Neglect of the flock may be due to busyness, or it may be due to procrastination. Respectful confrontation by the Shepherd is called for. The lay pastor is being tested as to how important the ministry is to him or her in light of God's call. The commitment to the Lord and His Church, sealed by the laying on of hands, calls the lay pastor to place a high priority on regular contact with his or her people. At times lay pastors may have to be held accountable—with respect, love and sensitivity, of course.

The words of Paul to Timothy will help in calling the lay pastor to a renewed commitment: "Hence I remind you to rekindle the gift of God that is within you through the laying on of my hands" (2 Tim. 1:6). By using this Scripture the lay pastors can see that they are in good company when called to a new start-up.

Now what do I do? A dilemma is faced by lay pastors who have neglected their flocks. They may be so out of touch, they are embarrassed or ashamed to break the prolonged absence by making a contact. What do they say to the people? How do they face them?

The longer they let it go the greater the feeling of guilt and the more difficult it is to make the contact. Honesty is the best policy.

"Hello, this is Steve Pearson. It's been a long time since you have heard from me. I'm your lay pastor, remember? . . . I want to apologize to you for not keeping my commitment. I fully intended to keep in touch. I feel bad about neglecting my pastoral duties . . . . I don't have any excuse. I guess my priorities got all fouled up . . . . Will you forgive me? I want to arrange a time to come to your home again. When will a visit work out for you?"

We counsel our lay pastors to contact their people by phone, make personal visits or write notes, so as to honestly admit neglect, ask forgiveness and renew their commitment to contact them regularly. We have found people to be understanding. Usually they have not felt as neglected as was perceived by the lay pastor.

Taking action. Marlene Wilson, in her book *How to Mobilize Church Volunteers,* asks the question: "If a volunteer goofs up, what should I do? Can you ever 'fire' them?"[2]

She firmly recommends these four action steps: *First,* you need to review the job description. Together, the shepherd or clergy and lay pastor need to look at the commitments taught in the Equipping Seminar and affirmed in the Commissioning. This first step will often be the only one necessary to take.

Second, clarify the problem and be explicit about your expectations. Talk together about the problem. Hear the feelings. Get the lay pastor's perspective on the reasons. Be empathic. Restate the expectations explicit in PACE.

Third, examine the alternatives together. These are: (1) to release the person from pastoring, (2) to renew the commitment, (3) reduce or restructure the flock or (4) other possibilities which would surface in the dialogue.

Finally, choose the alternative on which you both agree, and set a time line to implement and monitor the progress. Ask: "What is a date by which you could contact your seven families?" or, "It looks like you may have too many in your flock. Are there certain ones you would want to drop?" It will be important for the shepherd to give support and affirmation along the way.

To Marlene Wilson's four steps I add a fifth: *Pray.* Spend time together in the presence of the Great Shepherd. In your prayer: (1) acknowledge the Lord's presence in your talking together; (2) confess neglect and/or procrastination; (3) express gratefulness to God for the privilege of doing ministry; (4) renew the commitment, both general and specific; (5) depend upon the Holy Spirit for a fulfilling pastoral relationship and fruitful pastoral contacts, and pray, "Oh Lord, help me not to goof-off again."

Difficulty Number Four: People Have Problems You Cannot Solve

Like it or not, pastors (lay or professional) are not primarily saviors, rescuers or problem-solvers. Rather, each is a presence, a listener, a lover. There are problem-solvers to whom you can refer people when appropriate. The shocking fact that some churches have been sued because of their counseling people in trouble requires a lay pastor (or professional) to make referrals if and when necessary.

The simple guidelines we use are:

1. When there is serious illness contact the Minister of Pastoral Care or other staff.
2. When there are serious problems needing more than listening, being-with and prayer, contact the appropriate staff person.
3. When you encounter spiritual, biblical, moral questions, conditions or behaviors that need more than "being with," more than your answers or solutions, contact the appropriate staff person.

Even therapists, doctors and others in the helping professions encounter problems they cannot solve and refer their clients. The pastor is the one who is *with* people in their problems. Rarely is the pastor the problem-solver.

Even God does not solve all of one's problems. "I will be *with* him in trouble," God promises (Ps. 91:15). With the ultimate problem of death God only gives His pres-

133

ence: "Even though I walk through the valley of the shadow of death, I will fear no evil; for thou art *with* me" (Ps. 23:4). The point is that the pastor's role is more *presence* than *problem solving*. Many people have unsolvable problems. God plans that they not be alone in their problems but that He be with them in the person of their pastor. Remember the story of the frightened little girl saying, "I need love with skin on."

There is something about the nature of many of us that causes us to long to be problem-solvers. Just being with people, sharing their hurt, their grief, their disappointment, their disgust, does not seem to be doing anything. We think we must *do* something. Pastors have to learn that being with *is* doing something. Often the greatest appreciation is reserved for the one who was present with a person through troubles rather than to the one who gave advice or nobly tried to solve the problem.

Not a failure. Lay pastors should do as much as they can to solve a flock member's problem within the limits of their training and experience. However, instead of thinking they are failures because they cannot rescue, they need to understand that just by being there they have done all they could. They must not feel frustration or failure when they have turned their energies to being with, listening and weeping with those who weep. They can pray while they are standing by, silently or aloud. They can say, "I just want you to know I am with you, that I love you and that I care."

A clear example of not being able to solve a problem but of being with a person in his trouble is ministering to a person committed to jail for five years. You visit and pray for the person rather than release him or her. Another example is being with a terminally ill person. The pastor

134

will be present, not heroically to save the person from death, but just to be there. To do this calls for lay pastors to tolerate the reality of their own powerlessness while they are giving themselves to their flock members as a Christian brother or sister through whom God's gracious love and comforting strength can flow. It is as Juanita Ryan, a psychiatric nurse, professor and author, writes, "People in crisis need loyal friends more than they need experts."[3]

The story is told of a man seeking to console a friend who was in great sorrow.

"Let us pray right now that God will reach down and touch you and comfort you in your distress," the man said.

As the two bowed in prayer, the man put his arm around his troubled companion. His friend gasped and burst into tears.

"God touched me! I felt Him put His arm around me!"

Then he opened his eyes, and his countenance fell.

"It's only your arm," he said. "I thought it was God."

"It was God," his friend wisely replied. "He just used the arm that was nearest."

Those of us who pastor can seldom remove what causes the distress but we can often be the nearest arm.

Difficulty Number Five: Lay Pastors Experience Differing Degrees of Acceptance and Effectiveness in Their Ministries

"Three of my families have accepted us beautifully, but the other three just don't warm up to us. In fact, we feel like part of the family with the first three and like the ugly duckling to the others."

These variances are the realities of pastoring. Lay pastors must be ready to settle for different degrees of acceptance and effectiveness without withdrawing from those who seem aloof and unresponsive. They dare not become judgmental. They do not understand the nature of pastoring if they personally become offended when some in their flocks hold them at arm's length.

The people who do not accept the lay pastor with enthusiasm and do not indicate that he or she is effective, may actually need personal attention and faithful prayers more than the others. They require the agape kind of love—giving yourself to another regardless of the response. Jesus knew that only one of the 10 lepers would show appreciation for being healed, but he loved and healed them all anyway.

"I have faithfully prayed for the Bennets and have contacted them regularly but I don't see any results," David Jones observed. "They always seem friendly but after pastoring them for six years they still don't come to church regularly and they aren't growing spiritually. I'm about ready to give up!"

Samuel Southard's comment on this problem is that when lay pastors extend themselves to help others, it is very discouraging to be rejected or to recognize that people in need remain the same.[4] The lay pastor has to accept the varying degrees of acceptance and effectiveness as the nature of pastoring. They cannot always have warm fuzzies.

Difficulty Number Six: What Form Does Pastoring Take When There Are No Apparent Needs or Crises

Most people, most of the time, are not in crisis. The delusion of many lay pastors is that unless people are in crisis there is no need for pastoring. "These people don't need me. They don't have problems. Give me some people who need a pastor." The one who says this obviously has not grasped the basic concept of the Lay Pastors Ministry as expressed in PACE.

Different Forms of Pastoring. In noncrisis times pastoring takes the form of loyal friendship. Good pastoring represents Christ and helps develop a life of faith amid common circumstances. Please read this strong statement carefully: If we are not in touch with people in their everyday things, it means that we are not taking seriously what is happening in their lives most of the time.

Small talk, the meandering conversation that characterizes friendship and sets its own agenda, is the true expression of what is going on at the time. It is at these down-to-earth points where the lay pastor's life can gear into that of another's. If we do not engage in small talk we are left uninvolved with most of what is happening in people's lives.

The bonding of lives occurs in the little everyday things as surely as it does during a crisis. To engage people in heavy spiritual talk, help untangle some knotty problem, rescue from a crisis or give wise counsel takes a certain kind of artfulness. Loyal friendship and small talk also requires a certain kind of artfulness.

Noncrisis Initiative. Lay pastors need equipping in *noncrisis initiative.* The reason that it is a relatively simple pastoral act to respond to a crisis such as sickness, injury, loss of job, fire, death, and to such happy events as marriage, birth of children, graduation and birthdays is that these crises and events provide a very simple process: crisis and response.

There are these four elements in a crisis: purpose, time, notification and focus.

1. The *purpose* is identified by the need. For example, a person is rushed to the hospital. The purpose for a pastoral call is already identified.
2. The *time* is set. The person is in the hospital now.
3. You are *notified* of the crisis. Someone has given you the information to which you respond. There is nothing to initiate.
4. The *focus* is the crisis. Deciding what you will do, out of a wide range of possibilities, is narrowed for you. You will bring a sense of the presence of God into the room of a troubled person.

In initiating a noncrisis contact the lay pastor must do these same four things on his or her own initiative:

1. Identify the *purpose*. Examples may be:
   a. A desire to know the person better.
   b. "Touch base" to see if everyone in the family is okay.
   c. Talk about some matter of spiritual nurture.
2. Set the *time*. When there is not a crisis it is not urgent the contact be made today or this week. That is the problem. Without procrastinating you have to decide your own time and negotiate an appointment convenient to the flock member.
3. Take the *initiative* in contacting. The lay pastor cannot wait to be notified by the fam-

ily that they want a visit. It is very rare that a flock member will call a lay pastor unless there is a problem.

4. Establish the *agenda.* "I just stopped by to visit, to get better acquainted and to see if everything is going along fine."

Difficulty Number Seven: Some People Do Not Feel Pastored Unless the Ordained Clergy Pastors Them

"I know the Krugmans have visited me but I want to see one of the pastors." Either the teaching from Ephesians 4 about the saints doing the pastoring has not reached Mrs. Meister or, more likely, having heard it, she is not buying it. She has also said, "I appreciate my lay pastors. They are a fine couple. But when I need a pastor I want Dr. Kirk."

How do we solve this problem?

First, we need to be sure that we believe Ephesians 4, that God has called pastors and teachers to equip the laity for ministry. We are working God's plan. We are doing the ministry for which we were equipped. We need to be convinced of that.

Second, the leaders must keep working toward total church acceptance of the belief that God has called lay people to pastor and that His Spirit has given them pastoral gifts. This belief is accomplished by preaching, teaching and practicing. Consistent pulpit ministry goes a long way in creating a favorable climate for the acceptance of pastoring by lay people. Special classes and articles in the church paper will have a powerful impact in changing a clergy-only church to a ministry-by-all-the-people church. The preaching, teaching and writing will not do the job unless the clergy will be consistent in giving full support to their lay pastors.

Third, the official board of the church will need to take action declaring pastoring by lay people to be the way the church will pastor its people. This action should be well publicized after the structure has been created and the ministry is on line.

Firm and Consistent. The clergy, lay pastors and officers will have to meet the complaints of people by firmly stating that things are now different, that God is calling the Church to take Ephesians 4, 1 Peter 5 and other Scriptures seriously regarding pastoring. They have to stick with their decision in spite of the complaints. They will need to be patient, understanding and respectful, knowing that some people may never switch to authentic Spirit-led pastoring by lay people.

Exceptions. Two realities modify what may seem to be this "hard line." First, some older people will never feel pastored by anyone other than the ordained clergy. Love would call for a departure from the "hard line" to provide for pastoring by both the laity and clergy. We have found that many lay people have won older people over to their pastoring by prayer, love and faithful contacts while being simultaneously pastored by the clergy.

It is imperative in the transitional time that lay pastors believe themselves to be authentic pastors, called by God into the ministry. Lay pastors will also need to understand that many older people behave according to the principles of tradition so as not to equate nonacceptance with personal rejection.

The second reality is that the professional pastor will need to do the heavier pastoring. The model in Exodus 18 called Moses to handle "every great matter" while he

140

"chose able men" who would handle the other matters. Crises, critical illness, death, counseling and discipline are some of the "greater" matters to be handled by the clergy.

Deciding which matters are "great" and which matters are "small" depends somewhat on the gifts and experience of the lay pastor and the availability of the clergy. Establishing the dividing line is more of an art than a science, more subjective than objective. An open, communicative and mutually respectful relationship between lay pastors and clergy will enable this process to occur without feelings of failure, interference or rejection.

True or False. Before we leave this chapter on managing difficulties we need to look at five assumptions commonly believed to be true, which, if accepted, will lead to serious problems and weaken the Lay Pastors Ministry: Circle *T* if you believe the statement to be true; *F* if you believe it to be false.

T   F   1. Lay people can minister effectively without training and without continuing to be trained.

T   F   2. All committed lay people are strongly self-motivated and self-starters.

T   F   3. Lay pastors do not need affirmation, appreciation, guidance and correction (or they do not want it).

T   F   4. All committed people will come and offer themselves to be lay pastors without your seeking them.

T   F   5. The ministry, if blessed by God and set up properly, will be trouble free.

If you circled *F* for all five, you get an *A* +. They are all false. If any are believed to be true, pastoring by lay people is headed for trouble.

In conclusion, if managed well and if the false assumptions are rejected, difficulties will be turned into learning experiences. They will ultimately strengthen this God-given ministry. To struggle successfully with the difficulties rather than to be defeated by them will result in a more authentic and effective caring for God's people than if we did not have the struggle.

Identifying and managing the difficulties is imperative to the effectiveness, continuation and integrity of the ministry. We will now move on to evaluation by which we can deal with the weaknesses and be affirmed by the strengths.

Notes:

1. The notes are from my Doctor of Ministry final document, "Providing Adequate Pastoral Care to Every Member of the Church," 1979. It is in both the Doctor of Ministry office and the library of the United Theological Seminary, Dayton, Ohio.
2. Marlene Wilson, *How to Mobilize Church Volunteers* (Minneapolis, MN: Augsburg Publishing House, 1983), p. 95.
3. Juanita R. Ryan, *Standing By* (Wheaton, IL: Tyndale House Publishers, Inc., 1984), p. 188.
4. Samuel Southard, *Training Church Members for Pastoral Care* (Valley Forge, Judson Press, 1982), p. 26.

9

Evaluating the Ministry

During the era of moon shots, one vital phase was to monitor the flight direction. Periodically, it was necessary to make in-flight corrections of the rocket course so as to reach the exact spot of its planned destination.

Evaluating the Lay Pastors Ministry is the monitoring process whereby we check our distance and direction—our performance—in light of our goals for the purpose of making "in-flight corrections" as necessary.

We need to know four things:

1. Are we doing what we said we would do?
2. Are we having the results anticipated?
3. Are we using the methods we planned to use?
4. Do we need to make some changes?

If we are really serious about learning how the ministry is going we will need to ask two kinds of questions of the lay pastors:

143

1. How many contacts were you able to make last month?
2. How do you believe you are being received by your people as you contact them?

Number one is *quantitative,* counting the number of contacts. Number two is *qualitative,* trying to determine the character and quality of the relationship. Both kinds of evaluation are essential to feeling the pulse of the ministry. We need to know both quantity and quality—how much pastoring is going on and how well it is being done. Those who *run* the ministry need to know how it is going and those who *do* the ministry need to know how they are doing.

The quantitative and qualitative information will prove invaluable in evaluating the *purpose, goals* and *objectives* of the ministry. The following examples will help us distinguish between these three.

Purpose—To equip lay people for pastoring. A purpose is general and somewhat visionary.

Goal—To develop an equipping program by a certain date. Note that a goal is specific, achievable and measurable. One way of determining whether you have a purpose or a goal is if you can date it.

Objective—To schedule a series of classes on how to be a lay pastor. A second objective to be worked on at the same time might be to register 25 people for the first class. You can see that it may take many objectives to achieve one of the goals, which in turn fulfills the one purpose.

Objectives are set so as to achieve the goals. The goals in turn are established so as to fulfill the purpose.

The purpose is the vision. The goals and objectives are the action steps necessary to carry out the vision. Like a stream flows into a river and the river flows into the ocean, so the objective flows into the goal and the goal into the purpose.

Our *purpose* in bringing the Lay Pastors Ministry on line was to provide adequate pastoring for our members. One of the many *goals* was to create a course by which we could equip lay people to be pastors. One of the *objectives* which would help accomplish the goal was for me to do research on what should be in a course, write it up and submit it to the Ministry Group for their input and approval.

OUR FIRST EVALUATION

The ministry was launched. To find out if we were accomplishing our purpose we did an evaluation at the end of the first six months. We needed to know if the two assumptions underlying the ministry were valid: (1) Lay people can pastor effectively and (2) People will accept pastoring from their peers. The evaluation instrument was titled, "Christian Impact Sources" (see page 152). People being pastored were asked to rate, on a scale of one to ten, the impact seven sources of spiritual influences were making on them.

The results thrilled us! They validated the two assumptions we had made. Our purpose was being fulfilled. The impact of the lay pastors was rated the same as that of the senior pastor of the church. On the one-to-ten scale other staff rated one point less than the lay pastors. The other impact sources—radio/TV, books, magazines, tapes, neighbors and other churches—rated less.

145

No Threat

The senior pastor and other staff could have considered the results of this evaluation a threat to their professional image and integrity. Instead, the ministerial staff rejoiced in the development of this ministry and believes the results are indications that God called the ministry into existence. They see it as His answer to the need of giving adequate pastoral care to our membership.

To get a qualitative reading on the ministry we have done two major evaluations. (Copies of both evaluation forms are in the Leader's Guide.) One was from the perspective of the lay pastors; the other from the perspective of the people being pastored.

THE LAY PASTORS' PERSPECTIVE

The conclusions from the lay pastors' perspective are as follows:

1. Our ministry is about 70 percent effective; that is, seven out of ten families are being regularly contacted with a satisfactory degree of effectiveness. We felt this was an acceptable level of pastoring but we needed to find ways of improving that percentage.
2. We needed to find ways of affirming our lay pastors for their excellent quality of pastoring.
3. Some of our lay pastors need to be encouraged to pray with their people. We need to equip them to pray prior to the contact, to build a prayer out of their conversation and

to make the transition from conversing to praying.

4. Some of our lay pastors have difficulty knowing how to relate to people with whom they are unable to build a warm relationship. We need to help them know that the nature of pastoring is that some people are not going to warm up to them, but that God calls us to pray for them and care for them anyway.

5. Deliberate plans need to be made by the lay pastors to build a relationship with the children in their flocks' families.

6. Nearly 100 percent of the lay pastors read our monthly newsletter. We can discover more effective use of this medium of communication and equipping since it is being read.

7. We need to find ways of motivating our lay pastors to continue being equipped by providing books, tapes, special classes and some means of recognition to those continuing to be equipped.

8. We need to be more firm in requiring the monthly reports and, along with this, help the lay pastors to understand why the reports are important. The importance is that reports are one of the chief ways I have of keeping in touch with the ministry so as to know its strengths and weaknesses and who may need help in pastoring.

Christian Impact Sources

Influence On Our Christian Life Is From Several Sources.
Please Check The Impact The Following Sources Have Had On Your Spiritual Life
Ranging from *None* (1) to *Life-Altering* (10).

Source	1	2	3	4	5	6	7	8	9	10
Senior Pastor							✓			
Other Staff						✓				
Lay Pastor							✓			
Radio/T.V.			✓							
Books, Tapes and Magazines						✓				
Neighbors	✓									
Other Churches			✓							

Note: **When 75% of the people surveyed check "Lay Pastor" at 5 or higher, the Lay Pastors Ministry is "adequate."**

What we learned from the evaluation enabled us to make "in-flight corrections" so as to get to the destination we planned. It also made it clear that we must always be working at improving the ministry.

THE FLOCKS' PERSPECTIVE

We sent evaluation forms to two randomly selected members of each flock. We were looking for this kind of qualitative information:

1. How well people feel they are being cared for
2. The lay pastor's faithfulness in contacting people
3. People's desire for visits from lay pastors
4. The mutuality of the ministry
5. Significant experiences with their lay pastors
6. The decline or deepening of relationships
7. The most effective influences on their spiritual lives
8. Attitudes about the ministry as a whole.

70 PERCENT EFFECTIVE

We felt good about the results!

Again, our interpretation of the evaluation told us the ministry was about 70 percent effective. I have often made the statement in relation to this percentage that if you were to evaluate the pastoring of over 100 professional clergy and could come up with 70 percent effectiveness, it would be a surprise.

You might like to read some ways this sentence was completed on the evaluation form: The best thing my lay pastor has done for me is . . . :

- Remembering us on Christmas and birthdays.
- Calling me on the phone at a time of need.
- Showing me the right road to follow, a better relationship between myself and Jesus Christ.
- Listening.
- Showing interest in my well-being.
- Being my friend and convincing me to call her anytime I need to talk.
- Extending deep sympathy and help in my sorrow.
- Being a constant person to turn to. The clergy have no idea of the everyday crises and struggles and only come at extreme crises.
- She brought us a meal after our baby was born.
- Praying for my husband's job and mine.
- Making it plain to us that we are important.

Here are some of the responses to the part, I want to say this about the Lay Pastors Ministry in CHPC . . . :

- The concept of one-on-one pastoring is great.
- I could and would depend on my lay pastor for help at any time of need in any circumstance.
- I feel that they are always open and ready to listen to me and offer support.

- The value of this ministry is not easy to describe in words. It has been a one-to-one feeling, expressed in many ways to show that you are loved and that help is available at all times.

- From our experience, we cannot say enough good about the Lay Pastors Ministry. It has been very important in our lives. Our problems have been more dramatic than some, so our needs were greater. Our lay pastors were always there without having to call them or ask for help. Their love was unconditional and their faith unshakable.

- It has blessed me deeply and has also given me a new friend.

- It should be in place at all churches.

- I firmly believe in it.

- Due to the fact that our church is very large, lay pastors give the close relationships which would otherwise be lost.

- I think it is good for the church to have someone to look after the members both in a spiritual and personal way. It means a lot to me to have my lay pastor come to see me and to have someone to confide in.

The following responses from people being pastored caused us to work hard at improving the ministry:

- Perhaps the number of families given each lay pastor is too many. I don't know. Perhaps our

lay pastors have other families who take
much of their available time.

- The best thing our lay pastor did was to call
us and tell us his name. He asked where we
sit in church so he could meet us, which he
never did.
- The infrequent visit of my lay pastor is due to
his working schedule at the hospital (working
a lot of 36-hour shifts) and is no reflection of
his commitment or desire to serve. I understand completely and have no bitter thoughts
or hurts in the situation. I must also confess
that I have not prayed or supported him very
much or none.
- More care should be given in selecting lay
pastors and matching them to their "sheep."
- Our experience has been that the program
isn't for everyone. Some people are not gifted
to be lay pastors.

One of the toughest hassles for many lay pastors is the
monthly report. In spite of this, however, the report is
essential to the health of the ministry.

Quantitative evaluation goes on constantly via these
monthly reports. They tell how many contacts are being
made, what kind of contacts they are and who is making
them. We analyze these reports periodically to determine
if a sufficient number of home visits are being made in
comparison with other kinds of contacts. These reports
also become a means of affirming the lay pastors because I
or the shepherds respond to each one by mail or phone
call. Often problems surface in these reports which we try
to deal with promptly.

SELF-EVALUATION

We challenge lay pastors themselves to set goals for their pastoring. These goals, then, are the objective standards by which they can do self-evaluation. They can set a goal, for example, to deepen flock members' spiritual maturity in accord with Ephesians 4:12-14, "Building up the body of Christ . . . to mature manhood, to the measure of the stature of the fulness of Christ . . . that we may no longer be children, tossed to and fro and carried about with every wind of doctrine."

The objectives by which they can reach this goal might be:

1. Enable them to know God experientially—tasting of the goodness of the Word of God as stated in Hebrews 6:4,5. This image of sensory experience that conveys the reality of spiritual experience can be talked about during visits.
2. Encourage them to pray privately and with others.
3. Stimulate them to seek the guidance of the Holy Spirit.
4. Help them grow in their knowledge of Scripture.
5. Assist them in discovering their gifts for ministry, perhaps even the Lay Pastors Ministry.

VARIETY, THE SPICE OF EVALUATION

A formal, well-planned evaluation of the ministry as a

whole should be made at least once each year. Evaluation of each part of the ministry should be also made each year: equipping, communications, calling forth (recruiting), shepherds, reports, administration, quarterly or monthly meetings, etc.

There is need to vary the evaluation instruments considerably. At times evaluation can be done by making personal contacts or phone calls rather than using printed forms. It can also be done by calling the lay pastors together in small groups to discuss the state of their ministries.

Being able to evaluate a ministry assumes that its form is well developed.

10

In Search of a Form

W herever the grace of Christ is present it is in search of a visible form that will adequately express what it is." This observation by Avery Dulles in *Models of the Church*[1] makes having an organizational structure of some kind essential.

We tried to follow the architectural principle— "function determines form." First, we gave attention to what we needed to do—provide pastoring for every member. Second, we began to form the structure that not only would enable the pastoring, but also assure its continuation.

CIRCLE THEOLOGY

Our approach to leadership and organizational structure is based on what we call Circle Theology. Human relationships can be defined in terms of either ladders or circles. *Ladders* represent a hierarchical system of relationships; we've all heard the phrase "climbing the ladder." Circles stand for a mutuality between persons who

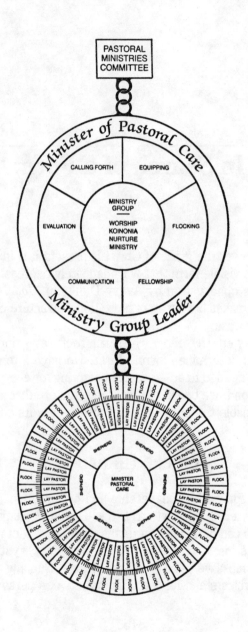

share, serve and submit to one another.

Circle theology is best expressed in the words of Ephesians 5:21, "Be subject *to one another* out of reverence for Christ," and Philippians 2:3,4, "Do nothing from selfishness or conceit, but in humility *count others better* than yourselves. Let each of you look not only to his own interests, but also to *the interests of others.*" As followers of Jesus Christ we are equals, sharing His love, His friendship, His teaching, His command *and* His ministry.

The preceding diagram depicts the organizational structure for our Lay Pastors Ministry. It says that we are committed to serve and submit to one another as we lead the ministry. Our first drawings were modeled after a conventional organizational flow chart showing a series of hierarchical relationships. Because we believe we are partners in ministry, mutually interdependent rather than certain people being over others, the circular drawing more adequately represents our relationships. Whereas the roles differ, the authority is equal and the accountability is mutual.

A GLOSSARY

Without intending to do it, we created our own jargon. Therefore, we developed a glossary to help you understand the terms used in the diagram. The words are very carefully chosen because we wish to clearly identify the designated roles. We believe that if we do not have the right word, it may be that we do not have the right idea. It is important to have the right idea so that the right work gets done.

Pastoral Ministries Committee—A committee of the official board of the church responsible for the pastoral

157

care of the church membership. In CHPC this "board" is the Session.

Ministry Group—12 to 16 people including the Minister of Pastoral Care who have ownership of the ministry under the authority of the Session. Though the group is brought together around the ministry, quality time is given at the meetings to worship, *koinonia* (sharing the problems and joys of our lives) and nurture (in the Lord and in the ministry). While putting the ministry together, we met semi-monthly. Now we meet once a month.

Calling Forth—This term is used rather than *recruit* or *enlist* to avoid the human-effort-only connotation characteristics of secular organizations. This term recognizes the participation of the Holy Spirit in calling people into the ministry. We neither twist arms nor apply pressure to get people to be lay pastors. We "pray . . . the Lord of the harvest" (Luke 10:2). Our personal contacts to talk with people about the ministry are not efforts to talk them into becoming lay pastors, but rather to alert them to the possibility that God is calling them into the ministry. One of the Ministry Group members has the responsibility of coordinating this phase of the ministry.

Equipping—This term describes the process of preparing people for pastoring. The common term *training* comes short of the biblical concept of "equipping" found in Ephesians 4:12; 2 Timothy 3:17 and Hebrews 13:21. The Spirit of God participates in the equipping so the person is equipped in faith, love, sensitivity, compassion and character as well as skills. As I elaborated in the chapter on equipping, lay pastors need to be equipped to *be* as well as to *do*. I have the responsibility of coordinating this phase of the ministry and doing most of the teaching in our equipping seminars.

158

Flocking—This refers to the activity of assigning members and their families to lay pastors. The total number assigned—between five and ten—is called a *flock*. A member of the Ministry Group has the responsibility for coordinating this phase of the ministry.

Fellowship—The lay pastors meet as a total group four times a year. The purpose of each meeting is fourfold: to worship, to equip, to share and to fellowship. We call this quarterly event *Lay Pastors Fellowship*. One member of the Ministry Group has the responsibility of planning and coordinating this. Another member plans the refreshments.

Communication—It is important to communicate with both the lay pastors and the congregation. A monthly newsletter, "The Shepherds' Call," goes out to the lay pastors. Regular articles appear in the monthly church paper. Even though this is the responsibility of a member of the Ministry Group, much of the work is done by church office staff.

Evaluation—Comparing the goals with what is actually done is evaluation. Formal check-up times are essential to determine whether what was planned is being accomplished. This phase of the ministry makes it possible to discover weaknesses and problems early enough to make changes before it is too late. A member of the Ministry Group is to develop evaluation instruments, initiate the process, interpret the results and recommend action to the Ministry Group based on the interpretation.

Lay Pastor—A nonprofessional church member who is called by the Lord (see John 15:16), whose call is confirmed by authorized people (see Acts 6:5) and who authentically cares for assigned people (see 1 Pet. 5:2).

Shepherd—The person who is a lay pastor to lay pastors, a resource person to them, and one who engages them periodically in "pastoral supervision."

The meanings of the following words, not part of the diagram but in the ministry, need to also be clearly defined:

Ministry—This is the activity in which a Christian engages in response to the call of the Holy Spirit and the Church. The term replaces what is commonly called *program*. Program has humanistic connotations, lacking the participation of the Holy Spirit and unique distinctiveness of Christ's Church. Every Christian is gifted by the Spirit for ministry and is therefore to be engaged in ministry.

Confirming—This is the act of accepting and informing an applicant of acceptance for lay pastoring. The Ministry Group is responsible for this. It is an important step in the process which the Holy Spirit uses to assure people who are being called to a particular ministry. Those who are not confirmed are helped to find another ministry or counseled on how to prepare for a ministry.

ROUND PEGS IN ROUND HOLES

In addition to the right word and its right understanding, we try to get the right person for the job at hand. For the Ministry Group this means we try to discover people's gifts so they can be doing that for which they are gifted rather than being assigned jobs just because someone is needed. In other words, we try to avoid putting square pegs in round holes.

OUR ABILITY TO CHANGE

A year after we began the ministry we made a major

change in our goal and structure. We feel good about our ability to change because often, after it has been created, the structure rather than the Spirit controls the ministry. Our structure originally provided a lay pastor for every member of our church. This goal was right and in most churches could be pursued to full implementation. However, because the other ministry areas in our church (evangelism, counseling, education, youth, children, missions and worship) provided for the pastoral care of the people doing those ministries, the leaders began to ask, "Why are you assigning our people to lay pastors when many people in the church are receiving no pastoral care?" Even though this problem may be peculiar to CHPC, it demonstrates the ability to not let a structure become a Frankensteinian monster.

After several meetings over a period of many weeks with the lay and staff people involved, we developed the structure pictured in the following diagram. Each ministry area, which has a lay person leading it and a staff member attached to it, is responsible to pastor the people involved in that ministry. They develop their own model for pastoring.

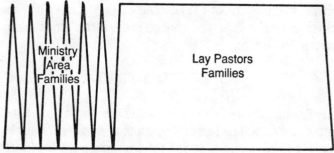

CHPC Comprehensive Pastoring Plan

161

The Lay Pastors Ministry coordinates the pastoring of the ministry areas and holds the leaders accountable. We do this by a system of reviewing the names of the people in the various ministries semi-annually (so people do not fall through the cracks when they move out of a ministry) and by meeting together occasionally for an interministry sharing of pastoring activity.

SOLID BUT CHANGEABLE

What we learned from this experience is that a ministry structure—the way the ministry is organized—is never to be set in concrete. But neither is it to be constructed out of sand. It needs to be solid, but not unchangeable.

The particular way a project is organized seems to take on a life of its own and fights for its perpetuation even to the death of the purpose for which it was created. Churches are especially susceptible to this fatality. They do not do too well in separating the form from the function. We believe we are continually open to organizational changes so the ministry can continue to be relevant. We want its purpose and spirit championed rather than its form. If the Spirit of Christ created the form, when the Spirit of Christ calls for a change in the form, we are committed to change.

FOLLOW THE TRAIL

At this place in the book, while we are talking about structure, it will be helpful to churches who want their lay people to be pastored to see the trail which will lead them from where they are to where they want to be.

1. Be convinced that God is calling your church to a Lay Pastors Ministry. This is done by prayer, serious discussion and study.
2. Create a context in which people will come forth to be lay pastors and in which others will receive their pastoring. This is done by preaching and teaching.
3. Secure the formal adoption of this ministry by the official board as the way the church will pastorally care for its people.
4. Bring together a group of six to sixteen lay people who have a variety of gifts, such as pastoral and administrative, who will commit themselves to bring this ministry into reality.
5. Worship, study, pray and plan together for at least six months before launching the ministry. The study should be of the Scripture, books related to the ministry and various models of lay pastoring.
6. Develop the theology, philosophy and structure. Get it into writing.
7. Do a pilot project for a six-month period to field-test your theology, philosophy and structure.
8. Call people into the ministry; then
   - equip them
   - flock them
   - commission them
   - supervise and support them
   - bring them together frequently for fel-

lowship, sharing, encouragement and
equipping.
9. Evaluate regularly.
10. Rejoice in the fruits of a Spirit-led ministry
which blesses God's people, both those
who pastor and those who are pastored.

Note:

1. Avery Dulles, *Models of the Church* (New York: Doubleday, 1974), p. 66.

11

What Lay Pastors Are Saying

E veryone needs pastoring at sometime—some more than others—and the church pastor can't be there for everyone," said one of our lay pastors. Having been the church pastor for years, I can say, "Amen" to that.

Churches that have not yet opened the pastoring ministry to the laity will be encouraged to seriously consider doing so by reading what lay people who are pastoring have to say. Churches in which lay people are already pastoring will be able to get new inspiration and practical ideas by listening to our lay pastors, as we would by listening to theirs. Hearing them makes authentic and effective pastoring by lay people believable. Their witness pricks the skeptics' three balloons: *doubt* about lay people wanting to take on the responsibilities of pastoring, *disbelief* that they can and *mistrust* of lay people doing authentic pastoring.

Admittedly, some professional pastors may be threatened by the depth of relationships that exists between lay pastors and their flock members, selfishly coveting that relationship for themselves. They believe that somehow the pastoral relationship is the divine right of the clergy.

But, once they give that right to the laity, they break into the new joy of equipping members of their church for pastoring. Their new excitement will be giving support to those to whom they have given the ministry.

The following are just a few of the statements by some of our lay pastors about why they believe in the Lay Pastors Ministry:

- I feel no one in the Body of Christ should go unnoticed, uncared for or unloved.
- It is Christ's design—people sharing gifts—none of us has it all.
- People need personal attention and care. Fellowship requires the Body of Christ to act, not just the ministerial staff—the "hired help."
- People need to know they are cared for in concrete ways, not just by hearing it from the pulpit.
- It's scriptural.
- In this day and age people are so transient and isolated. The family unit isn't as closely knit and supportive as it used to be or as God intended. So I feel lay pastoring helps fulfill this need as well as His commandment (see John 13:34, 1 Pet. 5:2).
- Pastors cannot possibly contact all of our people sufficiently.
- It benefits both the flock and us.
- In a large church it's easy to get lost. At least with a lay pastor there is someone.
- Lay pastoring gives me an opportunity to share my Lord. Persons may not always be

receptive, but my prayers are with them in the living of their daily lives.

- For singles, it is finding ways to touch base, not just by mail but personally, to let them know there is someone who cares about them.

Next are responses from some of our lay pastors when asked, "What do you find most satisfying about your pastoring?"

- Our flock accepted us and knows that we are praying for them and are available.
- I like having people that I am responsible for, even if it is just praying for them.
- Being able to reach out to other Christians on our own time schedule and being able to include our family in that ministry.
- I have gotten to know some very lovely Christians that I might not have. I have more people to love.
- Knowing I am serving the Lord in obedience.
- Having new friends in my life who show that they care about me, are glad when I call and thank me for my prayers and concerns for them.
- Seeing relationships grow, being able to make a difference, being used by God to bless someone.
- The blessings I receive from the relationships I have with my flock members.
- I am giving to other people and to our church. I've received so much from God and the

church; it's satisfying to be able to reciprocate.

- The joy of "fulfilling my ministry."
- The privilege of watching our flock members grow and being a part of the growth through modeling, praying and encouraging.
- Touching base with people I learned to love. Seeing change over a period of time (years).

Read on. Lay Pastors tell their greatest moment since beginning to pastor their people:

- When a flock member felt able to call us in a personal crisis.
- Seeing a person who had not been to church recently return to being a regular worshiper.
- Seeing a flock member come to know the Lord on her deathbed in the hospital.
- Being visited by all my flock while I was recovering from a heart attack.
- Being asked by a flock member to pray with the family in a small circle at the head of the coffin in a funeral home. I feel this was the result of having prayed with this person previously.
- A member of our flock was hospitalized with a kidney stone. His wife called and asked that I, as an elder, come and pray and anoint him with oil, which I did. When I called a few days later to discover how he was, I was told that, much to the doctor's amazement, no sign of the kidney stone remained.

168

- The experience, which remains as most memorable, is Mary's accident when no family could be found. The doctor and nurses were relieved in finding out something about her from me. It truly seemed God put me in that place at that time.
- We were pastoring an elderly lady who insisted she didn't need pastoring. She didn't want to "bother anybody" or "take up their time." On her birthday, as I was grocery shopping I found myself surrounded by flowers in a new section of the store. In a flash I knew what to do. I bought a handful of fresh-cut flowers and, within the hour, was at her house. She was able to receive this simple and spontaneous gesture and we spent two hours visiting. She did most of the talking.
- Being there for Barbie—sharing her growth in Christ.
- Six months after I became a lay pastor my mother was diagnosed with lung cancer. I was too upset and hurt to call my flock. Instead, I wrote them and most responded with letters of support, comfort, prayer and understanding. They saw my need, responded and, with God's help, carried me through that difficult time. Their letters were moving and uplifting.
- Seeing a lady laughing and talking with friends in the church courtyard after Sunday morning services one year after she told me that she didn't want anything to do with a lay pastor

and that she was shopping for another church.

- I cannot think of any time being greatest. Each time together our conversation on the phone is special.
- Having a three-year Bible study with one of our members.
- When, after five years of being put off, we finally succeeded in reaching one couple in our flock who agreed to spend an afternoon and evening in our home.

To balance this very positive record, we've listed some things lay pastors have found to be difficult:

- Keeping up with the monthly contacts in a consistent and a creative way.
- Making contact each month. We are busy and our flock seems to be on the go as well. There is a certain amount of pressure and guilt as the month draws to a close.
- The time crunch—making those appointments.
- Trying to have a personal meeting with flock [members]. People are so busy that it is hard to even schedule a half hour meeting. The flock does not want to give up time after working all day.
- Finding a way to reach flock members who won't meet us.
- To minister to one family who seems very self-sufficient at times but at other times has asked for prayer.

- Loving those who are, at times, unlovely and in need of our love the most.
- Being consistent in regular contact. I have to make myself do it. It does not come naturally.
- Praying out loud.
- Becoming intimate enough to know their needs so I can help without seeming to pry— genuine needs, not casual, superficial ones.
- Getting over my procrastination.
- My difficulties were timidity and hesitancy about calling and visiting. Thank God, they have been overcome.
- That I am not much help, or so it appears to me, but perhaps the Lord is using my feeble efforts and I am unaware.

As you have read, PACE (Prayer, Available, Contact and Example) is the backbone of the pastoring. The following are some of the thoughts and feelings our lay pastors have about these four parts of their commitment:

PRAYER

- The most important aspect of the program.
- Important! You become truly involved in the flock member's life as you pray for him or her. We have seen answers that allow us to rejoice with the flock member.
- I have to discipline myself to pray for my flock and myself as a lay pastor. I believe that it is only through prayer that I will become a better lay pastor.
- It's a privilege to pray for my flock. However,

I must confess this has not become a daily part of my life. I pray for them as God brings them to mind.

- It is so important to have each member of the church prayed for personally.
- This is the easiest for me, but I feel it is the most important because there is power in prayer.
- Something anyone can do anywhere and anytime.
- Prayer is the most important tool in lay pastoring. People appreciate prayers. They will give specific requests when asked.
- Very important and often the only way I can help. We pray for each other.
- The way it all really happens. The beginning, middle and end to receiving God's power in all that we do.
- It is important to let flock members know that you are praying for them.

AVAILABLE

- By being available we feel we let our flock know that they are really important to us and a top priority. I feel it is necessary to make myself available whenever a flock member needs me.
- I am always available and always stress this in letters, telephone conversations and meetings. I always include my address and telephone number with everything I write.
- This sounds easy, but not always so. It takes

172

scheduling, commitment and resolve.
- My people know that they can call me to take them on errands, arrange appointments, etc. They never have but they know I would.

CONTACT

- I depend upon the guidance of the Holy Spirit to help me determine the right time to call as well as what to say in order to bring about good rapport.
- I am still not comfortable calling all my flock members but try to do it every month. When I can't reach them by phone, I write.
- Some are easier to get in touch with than others.
- Contact is needed to help build relationships.
- Setting the time to contact is hardest. But once I get into it, I find it is a pleasure. Afterward it's a rewarding blessing.
- I feel the importance of contacting flock members regularly. Most seem to appreciate the personal visits.
- The real struggle, but necessary and rewarding after having done so.
- This is important to help the flock members grow spiritually and be nurtured at their own level.

EXAMPLE

- This is the hardest, but a good challenge to keep me growing.

- I just continue in regular worship and service believing that my flock will be positively led by my example of obedience. This is something I don't strive to tell them, but just let them see.
- This is important always as a Christian, a parent or a lay pastor. It lends credibility to that which you believe.
- What an encourager this concept has been, helping us to monitor our behavior as we see others watch us closely.
- This is the most difficult. In fact, I feel more "comfortable" in being an *encourager* to my flock.
- My example has not been so great. I have learned from some of their examples.
- I pray that I am a good example and that they will be understanding and forgiving when I am not.
- To be a growing Christian and example to my flock requires prayer, study and constant vigilance lest I fail to be what they expect. I thank God for His loving care and guidance.
- I don't feel I'm a great example biblically. I can't remember quotes from the Bible. But I'm a good listener.

Having heard from the lay pastors, let us now turn to those who are being pastored.

12

What the People Are Saying

The proof of the pudding is in the taste. And we were brave enough to test how this ministry was tasting to the people being pastored.

They had interesting, important and corrective things to say about their lay pastors and the ministry as a whole. To hear them is both an affirming and humbling experience. Some of their responses tell us that we do not yet have it all together. I have the feeling as I am writing that if through the years we had consulted more with those being pastored this ministry would be even more effective. Just their readiness to respond to the two statements we gave them to complete says a lot.

The first: I have found my lay pastor to be helpful in this way . . .

- He helped me to understand the workings of the church so I would know where I would best fit in to do my part.
- She is so very considerate and gracious

175

enough to say I have helped her. We have shared many gospel truths together.

- A good listener. Someone to "dump on" (important, especially for a single person).
- They are truly concerned and loving since my widowhood. Also warm, fun friends.
- We can share our thoughts, joys and sorrows with them. They are as close as family.
- She is a binding force between me and the church. She knows my needs and fills them.
- I know that she keeps me in her prayers regularly and she often is available to pray for me either on the phone or in person.
- Friends and relatives do not want to communicate regarding a terminal situation and a lay pastor fills these needs.
- Our backyard abuts that of my lay pastor. She can look over and see whether our lights are on or whether we are in the yard. If we appear not to be following our normal patterns she checks on us—gives us a call. This is comforting to us as old people.
- In giving me and my wife much needed help and assistance when needed.
- Periodically checking on us to see what our needs, both spiritual and practical, might be.
- Always available when needed. Emotional support.
- She phones me once in a while and brings me the booklet *Our Daily Bread* or leaves it on my enclosed porch.
- They have given me a lot of support on many issues, and I can talk to them any time.

- They pray for us and with us. We eat together several times a year.
- Always available when the need was greatest. Hospitalizations in particular.
- In letting me talk to her and she to me and praying together. I phone her and she phones me at times. We keep in touch.
- She has helped me by witnessing; by chauffeuring me to the veterinarian; by taking me shopping; by listening to me.
- I feel a genuine interest and concern from them and feel quite comfortable, if I needed help, calling them.
- I am very fortunate in having a wonderful son, although far away, and a niece and nephew in town who are very close to me and with whom I share my happy and sad and lonely times. But it is comforting to know that I could call on my lay pastor, as he has assured me I should, if I ever need him.

The second statement: In my opinion, the best thing my lay pastor has done is . . .

- We went to a picnic at their house. I felt quite comfortable throwing Kevin's bike in the car and asking Larry to fix it so he could "bike hike" with One Way Gang (the youth group). At Christmas, when I was not working, they gave us food. I was not offended. I know they were concerned about us. Actually, that food was our family's Christmas Eve dinner.
- Being my very best friend—someone with

whom I can relax. A Christian companion who is always available.

- Making me feel at ease with her and talking over problems. I loved her from the minute I met her.
- Checking on us regularly to see if we had any special needs.
- They counsel us.
- Always being affirming to me and always being down to earth while being a spiritual giant. To be my friend and in getting my husband and me into a small group.
- Being available; to pray with us whatever our needs.
- Listening. She is a wonderful listener. She also shares her life and problems with me so I feel needed by her. Our most joyous times are spent either at lunch together or on the phone.
- Giving me their personal friendship and love when needed most.
- Visiting us often when my husband was in the hospital having two hips replaced.
- Praying for me. At Christmas time she brought me a chrysanthemum plant.
- Shepherding me when the ordained pastors of CHPC are too busy to do so.
- During the time of my husband's illness and at the time of his passing, Bill's visits, calls and concern were greatly appreciated. It meant a great deal to my entire family.
- Adele is my lay pastor. Upon meeting we quickly became friends. In addition to praying

with and for me, she has been "God with skin on" to me in many practical ways. She helped me move to my new apartment. When my apartment was broken into and the intruder attacked me Adele rushed to my side to pray with me and comfort me. In a church as large as CHPC, the ordained pastors just don't have enough time to truly shepherd their flock while obeying God's call to new horizons. The lay pastor program fills the gap!

- After I found out who my lay pastor was, I phoned her and called on her first because she had had some surgery on her back.

Other miscellaneous tributes to their lay pastors include:

- We have found our lay pastors, Don and Ursula, to be *very special* people. They are loving, considerate in every way, fun to be with, gracious always. Although every lay pastor might not have all of these qualities, I would think all lay pastors would be very caring people to even make a commitment to this kind of ministry.
- Best friends can become even better through a lay pastoring relationship. My lay pastor was a good friend to begin with, even better now. We need each other more than ever because we are in this relationship.
- It makes me feel special, especially because he chose me personally to be under his care.
- I feel it is good to have another person's opin-

ion, as well as my own. (This person is single.)

- I also benefit by being available to her! It works both ways!
- I appreciate having someone to guide me according to biblical principles.
- My lay pastor is totally equipped and capable. A most significant factor. Everyone is not a qualified candidate. It takes more than enthusiasm and training. Personality and intuition are important.
- We have close phone contact and meet every two to three weeks. We both seem to look forward to this.

The following are some anecdotes I have recorded recently. If I had planned to record these through the years, I would have a voluminous and affirming log.

- This note was passed to me from a lay pastor via a friend: Florence King would like Communion at her house before April 1 if possible. She will leave for Florida April 1. She has bronchitis and other problems.
- A phone contact had been made by one of our 3-M ("Missing and Marginal Members"— inactive) phone teams because of declining worship attendance. This response was recorded: Records correct. Says she has been here only once or twice this year. Would like to find an apartment on this side of town, but it is hard to look while you are working. She says CHPC is her church and she hopes

to come back. She also says lay pastors are taking good care of her.

- A lay pastor to an 80-year-old woman took her home to introduce her to her husband so that rather than just "Bill," he would be someone with a face and personality. She has had her to her home occasionally since then. She takes her to the doctor regularly and helps her with groceries. This woman also feels free to call her when she has needs or when she feels she needs someone to visit with her.
- Alma's face beamed when I talked with her at a women's circle while telling me that her lay pastor had brought her the "biggest and most beautiful poinsettia that you could imagine."
- When I visited a member of our church in the hospital she asked how I knew she was there. When I told her I didn't know because all I had was the information on my hospital list, she said, "Probably my lay pastor, Bonnie Ewing, told you I was here." Then she proceeded to tell me that her lay pastor had brought a full meal to her home for her and her husband.
- Lay pastor, Ron Wolf, takes Fred White to a prayer group one morning each week. This is therapeutic for Fred as well as spiritually nurturing following his stroke many months ago.
- Lay pastor, Ruth Auburn, arranged for different people to take Jennie Smith's baby for two days while she was recuperating from the flu.
- Lay pastor, Linda Duncan, has become a special friend of an 83-year-old whom she never

knew before (Linda is only in her 20s). She asked me to send her a birthday card, assuring me it would be meaningful to her. She spent time with her celebrating her eighty-fifth birthday.

- A husband and wife had separated. Because of a stroke the husband's personality changed and prior negative characteristics were accentuated. The lay pastor prayed faithfully and remained in contact, giving spiritual and pastoral support to both. They tried both professional and volunteer counseling but were not reconciled by either. The lay pastor called me one day to ask if it was okay for him to refer them to a "no-nonsense" counselor, a friend of his. I assured him that it was, that he was their pastor. He made the contact. The following Sunday they were in church together, have been reconciled, and are living happily together again.

The ministry that has generated these testimonials will work in small and medium-sized churches as well as large ones. Those who wonder about that will want to read the testimonial from the pastor of a small church in chapter 14. But, before you do, read what other churches have to say about their lay people doing pastoring.

13

What Other Churches Are Saying

There's a call for you from Glendale, California."
"Hello . . . . Could you give your Lay Pastors Equipping Seminar sometime this spring to our deacons and other lay people? We want to start them in pastoring our people." One of our lay pastors and I spent a Friday night and Saturday equipping 30 members of that church. Pastors and lay people from other nearby churches were also present.

"Could you come for a weekend later this year or early next to lead a lay ministry workshop?" This letter was from the pastor of an 800-member church in Michigan City, Indiana, who wanted to start giving his lay people a vision for ministry. Four of our lay pastors and I made up the workshop team.

"We have 50 people ready to be trained to be 'shepherd helpers,' (lay pastors, in our vocabulary). When can you come?" We responded with a team of five. This church in Washington, D.C. was supplementing their group plan with one-on-one pastoring for people who were group resistant.

This phone call came from Seattle, Washington: "One of our lay leaders and I attended your seminar last fall. Since then we have been getting organized, and have a number of people ready to be trained to be lay pastors. When can you come . . . and can you bring one of your lay pastors along?" Two of our lay pastors and I spent a most productive Friday through Sunday there giving our 15-hour Equipping Seminar.

These are just a sampling of inquiries we have received and continue to receive asking for help in the training of lay people for ministry. Over the years several churches have adopted or adapted the model God has led CHPC to develop.

NATIONAL CONSULTATIONS

On three occasions staff members and lay people from these churches were invited to a National Leaders Consultation on Lay People in Pastoral Ministry. Churches that have only made inquiries regarding our Lay Pastors Ministry and/or have our Equipping Manuals and video tapes were also invited.

All three consultations were held in Cincinnati. I co-planned the first one with Rev. Jim Kenny who was at that time with Second Presbyterian Church in Kansas City, Missouri. At the second consultation, held June 1985, a task force of clergy and lay people was elected to plan a third. It was held June 27-29, 1986 and included both churches who have developed ministries and those wanting to learn. The consensus at the end of those three days was to continue meeting together. We believe the numbers of clergy and lay leaders desiring to participate in these consultations will increase.

Six questions were posed to selected clergy who attended the consultations:

1. *What Are Some of Your Thoughts About Lay People Being Authentic Pastors?*

- The New Testament recognizes the priesthood (pastorhood) of all believers. Therefore, God must have intended lay people to pastor. It is our task as leaders to help call their pastoring forth and develop it. Lay people certainly have the potential to be authentic pastors.
- Jesus didn't seem inclined to select any seminary graduates for his disciples. He felt 12 were plenty to look after. Few churches could hire enough pastors to meet that standard and I've always been a bit suspicious about paid lovers, anyway. Jesus set the pattern in Mark 6:7-13 and Paul theologized about it in Ephesians 4:7-12.
- I'm just overwhelmed by the caring, compassionate and very loving, patient work of our shepherds. It is sheer arrogance to believe our laity cannot pastor "as well as we pastors who have had all of the six hours of pastoral counseling classes required at seminary." More than arrogance, it is obstructionistic, selfish and negligent. Vital ministries are often overlooked or incomplete because the "poor, harrassed pastor has run out of time and

energy, giving himself sacrificially" when he should have been equipping the laity, God's people, for their ministries.

- They need to have a sense of calling and a realization that it is their responsibility to minister as an outgrowth of their commitment to Christ. They need to be trained and encouraged in their ministry. They need to be actively involved in developing the ministry as they see the needs to be met rather than being given a canned approach.
- It is biblical and effective as a means of caring for people. It is essential to give lay pastors the commissioning and authority to pastor, and to instruct the congregation about the biblical basis of lay ministry. A lay pastoring ministry must have a high profile if it is to be accepted by the congregation. Evidences and testimonies of effective lay pastoring must be publicly shared. It is important that clergy are secure enough to allow and encourage lay people to be pastoring the people. It is also important that they see it as their biblical function to train and equip them to exercise their gifts.

2. *How Capable Have You Found Lay People to Be in Pastoring?*

- Pastoring is, I believe, a spiritual gift. God did not choose to restrict this gift to seminary graduates. I often find laity to be more capable and/or gifted in pastoring than their preachers.

- In three years' experience I have found lay people to be every bit as capable as clergy in providing good pastoring. The recruiting of highly committed, deeply dedicated Christians who have caring hearts is essential. Training enables us to develop the capabilities we find already latent in these highly committed lay people.
- Our church has had mixed success with lay people in pastoring. However, on the whole, I would say that the lay people have been very capable in pastoring.
- I have found that lay people can be just as capable as we "professional ministers," depending upon their gifts, experience, motivation and equipping.
- Lay people are intelligent, able to accept responsibility, able to be spiritually mature, able to pray with others, diligent, able to keep records of visits and needs, capable of listening with a caring and responsive ear and mind, empathetic and able to exhibit a great deal of patience. These are all potential capabilities in the laity as they are in the clergy. These capabilities are no more built into one person, job description, or calling by ordination than are biblical knowledge, tenderness or discretion. Some are more apt. Some are,

187

by nature or temperament, more able to pastor than others, but the distinction is not ordination or non-ordination.

3. *How Effective Have You Found Lay People to Be in Pastoring?*

- As effective as their preachers encourage them to be, and often more so, in spite of their preachers' control needs.
- Their effectiveness does not depend on ordination. What pastoring does depend on is the heart and mind and inclination of the person—their love for people and their willingness and desire to bring people with their needs to the Lord.
- I have found the laity to be very effective in pastoring for several reasons: If they accept the job and are trained, they do make the time. They are there where the need is. And they often exhibit a patience, tolerance and empathy greater than any busy pastor.
- They have been very effective.
- I have found some to be very ineffective, but also some whom I consider to be very effective.
- The effectiveness of lay people is seen in the skills utilized, and the feelings expressed by the helpees who have received these trained helpers with enthusiasm and appreciation. A classic example of this is the flock-tender (lay pastor)

whose flock member called recently from the hospital to ask her to stop by and see her since she had a tentative diagnosis of cancer. She wanted to discuss her condition with her lay minister. This was done even before the clergy was aware of this person's need. The flock-tender went to her, listened sensitively to her, has stayed closely involved with her and has kept me fully abreast of any developments. The cancer victim is at home and stable and can't say enough nice things about the dedication of her flock-tender.

4. *In What Ways and to What Extent Do People Accept Pastoring from Lay People?*

- If people are receiving quality, Spirit-filled care they don't care much about the form or source. If they aren't receiving quality care they will be angry about whatever is going on, lay or professional.
- I believe that people accept pastoring from lay people to the extent the leadership of the congregation is committed to that philosophy and the extent to which the lay pastors earn it. Juan Carlos Ortiz said, "The job of the lay pastor is to steal the sheep from the preacher." This can be done over time when shepherds genuinely try to develop rapport.
- In those areas where the pastor cannot consistently spend time pastoring and

189

where people do not have expectations that the pastor should do that, then people are willing to accept pastoring from lay people.

- There is a re-orientation process necessary for people to both believe in and accept lay pastoring. We accomplished this by way of making introductions in our new members classes. There the shepherds meet their new parish members face-to-face and the whole parish program is explained by the committee. Pastors still should attend to hospitalizations and crises but not as the sole respondent.

5. *What Problems Do Lay People Have in Pastoring?*

- *One:* jobs. *Two:* families. *Three:* cultural practices that are preventive (i.e. the clergy/laity dichotomy). *Four:* procrastination—lack of motivation to activate the ministry at the end of a lay person's working day. *Five:* personal beliefs that they are not pastors and that they really can't do that work.
- The same ones preachers do. You can't give what you don't have. Caring is a phenomenon of abundance. If we love God with all we've got we can hardly hold back the rivers of living water He pours through the channels of our lives.
- Sometimes they, too, like the pastor, are

190

overwhelmed by the grief and loss and pain of those for whom they are caring. Sometimes lay pastors neglect their own walk with the Lord, and thus their own renewal of spiritual, physical and emotional reserves. Some laity have difficulty with particular aspects of visitation (i.e. hospital). Shepherding dear friends through crises is very demanding and draining.

- Lacking confidence that they can pastor, being unaware of what their gifts are, lack of commitment to the ministry. Lay people who are not prepared or qualified to do a particular ministry give those in their groups a bad exposure to lay people pastoring.

6. *Have You Found the CHPC Lay Pastors Model Useful?*

- Yes. While we have not yet taught it, we will be teaching it in the fall. We know it to be a model similar to that which we will be continuing to use. The structure is a good structure but must not be made too multi-level (lay pastors—shepherds—clergy) or it gets to be clumsy.
- Our church copied the model and in about three years had a caring ministry program involving 300 people in ministry.
- We have borrowed heavily from the CHPC lay pastors model, and even though

191

we have adapted it considerably, we are grateful for the development of the model.

- Yes. Primarily the equipping seminar, "calling forth" ideas, printed materials and ministry groups. We have adapted the equipping manual and some of the literature to our use as well.

- Yes! For the past several years I have inquired and researched into pastoral caring strategies other large churches are using and have received some interesting responses. Several had zone/district plans. Others did informal caring, such as people ministering to people as needs become known. My conclusions are that the zone/district/shepherd plans work admirably on paper but, for most churches, are practically ineffective in ministry. The reason is that these plans are based on an administrative role or geographic affinity. Another is the cell group model wherein a whole congregation is divided into cell groups. All members are expected to be active and participate. The virtue of this type model is that the real ministry takes place in the cell group. In reality, however, a significant number of people do not participate, leaving many people unshepherded. CHPC combines the best of all options. Administratively, it is efficient and effective. It is a ministry based on personal care and relationships. It can function as a cell group, but success is not determined by that.

How exciting it was to me and to the Ministry Group to receive these responses! Now read on for the testimonial of the pastor of a small church in Bellbrook, Ohio.

14

What the Pastor of a Smaller Church Is Saying

Written in May 1985, by Rev. Thomas Parrish,
Pastor of Bethel Evangelical Lutheran Church,
Bellbrook, Ohio.

As I survey my congregation of 230 members, from all walks of life, I am often overwhelmed by the need for ongoing ministry.

Christians are like automobile engines, constantly in need of a tune-up! The tune-up I am referring to is an ongoing ministry based on the PACE formula (Pray—Available—Contact—Example).

Traditionally, the formula of the Church has been the emergency-room approach. Those who are in immediate pain receive ministry; those who are not in imminent danger are determined to be healthy and do not receive Christ-centered ministry beyond Sunday worship. In my way of thinking, this approach spells disaster and needs to be changed.

THE NEED IS REAL

Over the past seven years, at Bethel Evangelical

Lutheran Church, I became increasingly aware of the need for Christians to minister to Christians on a regular, ongoing basis. The words of Saint Paul in Ephesians 4:11,12 became the theoretical basis of our ministry. When I say "theoretical" I mean that we agreed as leadership of Bethel that Saint Paul was right in saying the role of the pastor-teacher was to equip the saints (laity) for the work of ministry. The problem was that we didn't know how to get from theory to reality. We needed a functional basis for Christian ministry that aligned with the words of Paul.

BEGINNINGS

Approximately 18 months ago, I attended the *Helper* Evangelism Clinic at College Hill Presbyterian Church. It was at that clinic that I met Dr. Mel Steinbron. I remember him challenging the pastors to establish an ongoing Lay Pastors Ministry within their congregations.

Without lay pastors meeting the daily needs of members, our evangelism efforts would become a revolving door. As soon as we brought them into the church they would go right back out unless they were ministered to and given opportunities to minister in Christ's name. This made a great deal of sense.

I was aware of this problem at Bethel and heard other area pastors complain about similar problems. How do we keep our members once the honeymoon period has worn off? Dr. Steinbron's ideas and practical approach was the first logical and workable method I had come across. At that moment I knew that theory was suddenly becoming a channel of reality.

In the months that followed that first meeting with Mel Steinbron, I began to share the idea of lay ministering with the leadership of Bethel. I pointed out that lay ministry needed to go beyond participation in worship services and fellowship activities. Lay ministry should and could meet most of the real day-to-day needs of Christians. If lay people were trained and given real opportunities to minister to the emotional, spiritual, physical and intellectual needs of fellow Christians, we would begin to fulfill Jesus' command through Paul to "carry each other's burdens" (Gal. 6:2, *NIV*). We could, therefore, begin to love one another in very practical ways.

In September 1984, I phoned Mel Steinbron and began to make arrangements for further gleaning of ideas and means of putting the Lay Pastors Ministry into effect at Bethel. We invited Mel and lay pastors from College Hill to present their ministry to Bethel. Over 40 members of Bethel attended this special afternoon seminar.

A MINISTRY TAKING SHAPE

I watched the excitement grow as Christians young and old began to realize the potential for such a ministry at Bethel. Mel was also pleased, and invited us to attend their equipping seminar the following month. The arrangements were made, and six members of Bethel and I attended the Lay Pastors Equipping Seminar at CHPC.

The Equipping Seminar was a good overview of the Lay Pastors Ministry. The biblical need was well established, and practical approaches were shared. The weekend provided a solid basis for establishing what we would call a *Lay Ministry Program* at Bethel.

Upon returning from CHPC we met to discuss the nature and need of establishing a systematic lay ministry program for our church. Several were sold on the idea

197

immediately and wanted to get right at it. Others were hesitant and wanted to proceed slowly. One person felt that lay ministry would not readily be accepted by the members of Bethel. We agreed together to proceed with prayer, study, sharing and "trial families" to whom we would minister.

At the same time, Bethel was conducting a new members' class. The class was for anyone desiring to know more about our church and desiring to become part of Jesus' mission. The class consisted of 10 families. All eventually joined our congregation. The lay ministers decided that this would be a good place to begin experimenting with ministry. After prayer, I assigned two families to each lay minister. They were to use the PACE formula and make immediate contacts with these new members. During the new members' class, I presented the need for lay ministry and assured the class they would be contacted by their lay ministers shortly after joining Bethel.

THE FIRST PASTORAL CONTACTS

All the lay ministers plunged into contacting, and began to minister to their families within two weeks after their assignment. The first contact was in the homes of the new members, with the lay pastor explaining the Lay Ministry Program.

At first, some lay pastors were met with skepticism. This was a new concept for most of the new members but they were open to trying new things in a new church. Other lay ministers were met with open arms and were literally overwhelmed with acceptance and love. One lay minister was about to be plunged into being a servant and shepherd for Jesus Christ faster than any of us ever thought.

Within a few weeks of the first home introduction of the Lay Ministry Program, a nephew of one of the new members was involved in a very serious auto accident. When the bad news arrived, the new members immediately called their lay minister, seeking guidance and help. They shared with their lay minister that their nephew was close to death after having been crushed by the auto he was driving. This young man's parents were not professing Christians and were devastated.

The lay minister went to the hospital prepared to invite this young man to know Jesus and to minister to the entire family. After only a few minutes at the hospital, it was obvious the parents of this young man were resentful and bitter that a lay Christian had come to minister. They were especially angry at the Church which, they felt, had not met their needs in the past. So, why now?!

The lay minister felt a great deal of frustration as she attempted to minister in this context. As the weeks and months passed, she remained faithful in her visits to the hospital, ministering to the new members and the parents of this young man. It was truly an ongoing ministry that included baby-sitting, driving people to and from the hospital, praying and talking until late in the evening.

As of this writing, the young man has gone home, but awaits many plastic surgeries for the repair of his body. The new members who were ministered to have begun to minister themselves to others as they watched the modeling of ministry by their lay minister. Even the young boy's parents became aware of a miracle in the consistent love of this lay minister.

LAY PEOPLE CAN PASTOR

This example of lay ministry is certainly not the normal experience of those in the program. What it showed us is the fact that lay people can minister effectively to other lay people in the most difficult circumstances of life. It can happen with good training and a willingness to be used by Jesus Christ.

SHARING EXPERIENCES

Once a month the lay ministers and I meet together. At these meetings we look at Scripture, discuss our joys as well as our frustrations, pray, minister to one another and plan for incorporating more lay people into the Lay Ministry Program. At these meetings a variety of feelings are shared concerning their experiences.

Procrastination

The Lay ministers all agreed their worst enemy was procrastination, putting off that phone call or visit with the families under their care. Generally they found the contacts to be joyful but difficult to get around to on a systematic basis. Then they began to experience a sense of guilt for not having made more contacts within that past month.

One lay minister made a most interesting comment. He stated that he had come to see there was a big difference between being a Christian who witnesses and serves and being a Christian lay minister who is responsible for the care of those in his flock. This particular lay minister cares for two families in the congregation but has already begun to sense the joy and burden of caring for the spiritual well-being of others.

Bonding

They also began to experience a process of bonding. As they shepherded the families within their flocks they came to know them as individual people. They came to know where they worked, their hobbies and their needs. They began to enjoy each other and desired to know each other beyond the morning worship setting. Instead of *knowing about* each other, they began to *really know* each other.

The Squeaky Wheel

We also discovered that more and more people were open to lay ministry, both being ministered to and ministering to others. As one of the members of Bethel stated: "The squeaky wheel always gets the oil, but those who don't squeak need oil, too."

Many Christians at Bethel seem to be open and expectant of being included in a lay ministry family. Their needs are not gigantic, but they are real. They need the love and acceptance that can come only from others who get close to them and get to know them personally. As they are ministered to a multiplication effect begins: they, in turn, begin to look for ways to minister to others. The key to the process is consistent contact and ministry by the lay minister, which results in the effective care of those receiving ministry.

THE AUTHORITY TO GO AND MINISTER

In the seven years I have been preaching and teaching at Bethel I have continually repeated the theme of ser-

201

vanthood. I have encouraged Christians to care for one another. As in every congregation, there are some who attempt to meet automatically the needs of others on a regular basis. The vast majority would like to offer service and ministry in Christ's name but lack the courage and confidence to step out on their own. We have discovered that those involved in our Lay Ministry Program, under the authority of the church, take the needed authority to go and meet the needs of those in their care.

Even though they had heard the message of servant-hood for years it was not until they came to recognize that they had the authority in the name of Jesus that they began to involve themselves in the lives of others in practical ways.

I have come to realize this is one of the key elements for ministry—the *authority* to do the work of Jesus Christ. Those of us who are ordained pastors and have been set apart in some official capacity, may fail to understand the dynamics of this authority. We assume, and rightfully so, we are "called" to leadership and vision by the Lord Jesus Christ. We occasionally run into conflict with members who do not share the same vision, but we hold great power by the fact that we have been ordained and called to preach and teach. At the same time, the lay ministers are in need of public authority in the name of the church in order to assume the responsibility for pastoral ministry.

This became apparent to me shortly after my first meeting with the lay ministers at Bethel. Two questions were posed. First, when would they be publicly "called" into this ministry before the congregation? Second, when would they be given some form of identification authoriz-ing them to minister in the name of the church?

It was obvious they needed a public pronouncement of

authority to begin this ministry. In our situation we have purposefully postponed publicly giving authority to this ministry before the congregation until we have confidence in the details of this approach. On the other hand, I did present this ministry and people to the church leadership, who affirmed the authority and nature of lay people doing pastoral ministry.

A SYSTEMATIC APPROACH

"Why do we need an organized program of Christian ministry in the church when people are already caring for one another's needs?" This was a legitimate question posed to me when we first initiated the Lay Ministers Program. The question was accurate in stating that ministry and service were already going on at Bethel. The question was inaccurate in assuming this ministry was selective toward specific members.

The need for a systematic approach to lay ministry and caring for the needs of one another became apparent when several members experienced deaths in their families. One member was prominent, involved and visible in her activities. When a member of her extended family died many members of Bethel took time from work to attend the funeral, which was conducted across town in another Christian congregation. A second prominent member also experienced a death in the family and the same outpouring of love and ministry was apparent. A third member, less prominent, somewhat of a problem in the past, lost a family member in his extended family. Not one member of Bethel visited the funeral home or attended the funeral service. This was a deep blow to me as the pastor of Bethel.

I recognized that, unless we were organized to minister systematically and given specific responsibility for the spiritual care of all, some would be overlooked. The words of Jesus in Matthew 25:45 are straight to the point: "I tell you the truth, whatever you did not do for one of the least of these, you did not do for me" (*NIV*).

Someone might argue that such a systematic approach is artificial and phony. That is always a problem in any organized approach to ministry. But phoniness can happen whether we are organized or unorganized. Jesus' command for us to give *agape* love means that we care about the needs of others whether our emotions agree with us or not. The lay ministers are discovering that genuine emotion comes through obedience—rarely does it precede obedience. When we determine to minister to the needs of all members, a genuine bond of love grows between those interacting in Christ's name.

A systematic approach to ministry can be implanted at any time in any congregation that is committed to doing so. Bethel is in a very good position to provide lay pastoring for each member, since our membership is 230. All new members will automatically be incorporated into ministry families upon reception into the church. Our approach for those who are already members is based on need and openness to this ministry.

WHO IS TO BE INCLUDED

Some individuals are in unique situations such as single parents, divorced, aged, widowed. Those individuals will be the first to be included. Our prayer is that these people will be included in ministry families by the end of this year.

At the same time, we will incorporate individuals into a

ministry family when we discover their openness to lay ministry. Recently, one of our lay ministers approached me about a young woman in our congregation who expressed a need for ongoing pastoral care. She is new to Christ and the church but is rapidly maturing in her faith, witness and service. She recognizes that she needs guidance and support since her husband is not a professing believer. We immediately worked her into a ministry family.

The lay minister has been faithful in ministering to her needs and has taken this as an opportunity to minister to the entire family. This lay minister has stopped by the house and has spoken to the husband on several occasions. Recently the woman shared with me that her husband is opening up to the lay minister in a way she has never seen him open up to anyone else. We pray for a good outcome to this ministry.

OUR THREE GOALS

Our goal for lay ministry at Bethel is threefold. First, we want to fulfill Ephesians 4:11,12. We desire to equip the saints for the work of ministry. We believe this can be accomplished when we provide the opportunity for meaningful, life-changing ministry. The purpose of all our study and training is to enable each believer to truly represent Christ to those in his or her midst. We desire that this comes to pass with both hands and feet of action as well as words of love and comfort.

Our second goal is to meet the real needs of Christians on a daily basis. This ministry is one-on-one. Bethel is a small congregation of 230 members. As the solo ordained pastor under the old model of ministry, I would have to visit and speak to each person once or twice a week to accomplish the same output as the lay ministers. That would be 230 one-on-one contacts per week! In family units that would be 80 contacts a week!

No wonder families fall through the cracks and become discouraged with pastoral leadership when ministry is confined to one individual. The Lord Jesus had a much better plan of training 12, in depth, who in turn trained and ministered to others, who in turn followed that pattern of ministry.

Our third goal is to make the church a family instead of a fast-food chain. It is too easy for the church to become a spiritual food dispenser. People drive up on Sunday morning, place their order for quality music, entertaining preaching or baby-sitting, pay their bill and drive away. When the church down the street offers a new entrée, the car caravan goes there the next Sunday.

This approach and mentality is not a family! Jesus has called us to be family; we are related by the shed blood of our Lord and Saviour Jesus Christ. Only in small groups such as the lay minister and his flock can a family atmosphere be built. This small family is always directed to be part of the larger family in the local church and the extended family in Christ worldwide.

At Bethel we believe these three goals are reachable and functional under the guidance and love of Jesus Christ.

The Author's Note:

This report bears witness that churches of every size need pastoring by lay people and, if there is a will, this is the way. It also witnesses to the need to adapt our model (if our model is to be used) to the local context.

You have noticed that the lay people involved in the caring ministry in this church are called *lay ministers* not *lay pastors;* also that their ministry is designated *Lay Ministers Program;* and that they are starting with less than our minimum of five families per person.

Their adaptation of our model demonstrates that the principles of ministry in this book, not necessarily the form of ministry, can help any church have an effective pastoring ministry carried on by the laity.

Conclusion

We observe that God is doing a new thing in His Church around the world, that is, opening the pastoring role to lay people. We believe God called us to develop the Lay Pastors Ministry and that His Spirit has guided the principles of our structure. To us, the effectiveness of this ministry confirms the Spirit's guidance. Further confirmation is the number of other churches inquiring about it, inviting us to equip their people, attending our Equipping Seminars and adopting/adapting our model.

My expectations are two: (1) that the steady stream of churches adopting or developing lay pastoring models, such as ours, will become a torrent; and (2) that the National Leaders Consultation on Lay People In Pastoral Ministry will become an international network of churches who believe lay people are pastors too, and will come together to learn from and encourage one another.

I am, at the same time, humbled and thrilled to have been able to put in writing that which has been "love with skin on" in College Hill Presbyterian Church now for some eight years. I believe this book is truly a "how-it's-being-done-and-you-can-do-it-too" book.

Clergy and laity, get together. And in the power of the Holy Spirit, go for it!

Bibliography

Campbell, Alastair V. *Rediscovering Pastoral Care*. Philadelphia: The Westminster Press, 1981.

Collins, Gary R. *The Joy of Caring*. Waco, TX: Word Books, 1980.

Detwiler-Zapp, Diane, and Dixon, William C. *Lay Caregiving*. Philadelphia: Fortress Press, 1982.

Feucht, Oscar E. *Everyone a Minister*. St. Louis: Concordia, 1974.

Garlow, James. *Partners in Ministry*. Kansas City, MO: Beacon Hill Press, 1981.

Grantham, Rudolph E. *Lay Shepherding*. Valley Forge, PA: Judson Press, 1980.

Haugk, Kenneth C. *Christian Caregiving: A Way of Life*. Minneapolis: Augsburg Publishing House, 1984.

Heusser, D. B. *Helping Church Workers Succeed*. Valley Forge, PA: Judson Press, 1980.

Menking, Stanley J. *Helping Laity Help Others*. Philadelphia: Westminster Press, 1984.

Pohly, Kenneth H. *Pastoral Supervision*. Houston: The Institute of Religion, 1977.

Ryan, Juanita. *Standing By*. Wheaton: Tyndale House, 1984.

Southard, Samuel. *Comprehensive Pastoral Care: Enabling the Laity to Share in Pastoral Ministry*. Valley Forge, PA: Judson Press, 1975.

————. *Training Church Members for Pastoral Care*. Valley Forge, PA: Judson Press, 1982.

Stedman, Ray C. *Body Life*. Ventura, CA: Regal Books, 1979.

Stone, Howard W. *The Caring Church*. San Francisco: Harper and Row, 1983.

Tillapaugh, Frank R. *Unleashing the Church*. Ventura, CA: Regal Books, 1982.

Ver Straten, Charles A. *How to Start Lay Shepherding Ministries*. Grand Rapids, MI: Baker Book House, 1983.

Wagner, C. Peter. *Leading Your Church to Growth*. Ventura, CA: Regal Books, 1984.

Wilson, Earl D. *Loving Enough to Care: It Could Change Your Life*. Portland, OR: Multnomah Press, 1984.

Wilson, Marlene. *How to Mobilize Church Volunteers*. Minneapolis: Augsburg Publishing House, 1983.

Yohn, Rick. *Discover Your Spiritual Gift and Use It*. Wheaton: Tyndale House, 1982.

The publishers do not necessarily endorse the entire contents of all publications referred to in this book.

Leader's Guide

for

CAN THE PASTOR DO IT ALONE?

A MODEL FOR PREPARING LAY PEOPLE FOR LAY PASTORING

Leader's Guide Orientation

The book *Can the Pastor Do It Alone?* was designed to be a complete manual with which to equip lay people for pastoring. This *Leader's Guide* is to be used by the person doing the equipping. It is an essential companion to the book for the equipping process. The person who is teaching will be referred to as an "equipper" in this guide, consistent with page 93 in the book which lists "pastors and teachers" as equippers God has provided. It is important for the equipper to know he or she is a gift from Jesus to the "saints" being equipped. Knowing this makes the equipping seminar a burden of joyful responsibility for the equipper.

To conduct a successful seminar you will want to follow these recommendations:

1. Read the book through at least twice so as to become well acquainted with its content.
2. Read the *Leader's Guide after* becoming familiar with the book. The point is: know both the book and guide as thoroughly as possible prior to the equipping seminar. To know the contents of both will take weeks of reading, reflecting, discussing some of it with those close to you, collateral reading and much praying. If you will pay the price of time and energy you will receive generous dividends during and after the seminar.
3. Provide one book for each participant in the equipping seminar. Husbands and wives could share a copy in order to cut expenses but it is desirable for each to have his and her own copy. Usually, people do not mind being charged for the book. In some cases the church may

want to pay a part or all of the cost.

4. Request participants to read and study the book prior to the seminar.

5. Set the equipping seminar dates at least three months in advance of the event. This allows sufficient time for:

   • thorough preparation by the equipper
   • calling forth people to be equipped
   • making arrangements for facilities, equipment and meals.

6. The number of hours for the seminar should not be less than ten—more if at all possible. These should be spread over two days or an evening and a day. The ideal plan would be to have a weekend equipping retreat.

7. Keep the seminar on schedule. This will be one of the most difficult requirements of the equipper but it is one of the most important. When you give five minutes to the groups for discussion, cut it off at the end of five minutes, giving a warning after four minutes. When you have 20 minutes for a presentation, plan so you will have it completed in 20 minutes. *Use a timer.* If you do not run on time you will not be able to cover all that needs to be covered to adequately equip the people.

8. There will not be time to thoroughly teach, discuss, apply and assimilate all of the material in the book, nor to do all the "laboratory" experiences in the Leader's Guide. You will need to determine prior to the seminar which parts you will deal with lightly and which parts will require more time. In other words, you will need to pick and choose because of time constraints. Be prepared to make time adjustments as you move through the seminar. The parts you omit can be covered later in a monthly newsletter and/or subsequent equipping sessions.

9. Other tips on planning an equipping seminar:

   a. Be sure to take time to deal with people's questions. Encourage people to ask questions during the presentations as well as after each session.

b. The equipper should be available to talk with participants about their concerns and questions during refreshment breaks and other free times.

c. Start on time! End on time! This helps to build the integrity of the seminar.

d. Have a small task force handle arrangements for equipment, materials, registration, refreshment breaks, meals, lodging, etc.

e. The equipper should plan to build expertise in leading the seminar. If you have not done such a thing before, you may need to be patient with yourself. You will become more effective each time you do it. Many clergy and laity are not experienced in this role and will find it challenging to grow in the skill of equipping.

f. Utilize people with teaching gifts to teach parts of the seminar. When you get a Lay Pastors Ministry "on line," lay pastors can share their experiences in the seminar.

10. You will want to familiarize yourself with the sample forms and other material in the Appendix of this *Leader's Guide.*

11. During the seminar you will want to challenge the participants to continue their equipping after they have begun their pastoring and continue it through the years. See *The Three Levels of Equipping Lay Pastors* in the Appendix.

12. Near the end of the seminar you will want to announce the date and hour of the commissioning and give other data regarding the ministry.

Introduction to the Equipping Seminar

1. Assemble the participants at the scheduled hour.

2. Welcome the people. An official greeting from the senior pastor, committee chairperson or board representative would be in order.
3. Review the schedule.
    a. Tell what they can expect, including the evaluation at the close of the seminar.
    b. A sample schedule is included in the Appendix. This was used for one of our equipping seminars.
4. Worship with singing, a Scripture reading and prayer.
5. Get acquainted. Divide into groups of four or six. Within each group go clockwise, starting with the one whose name begins with the letter nearest the end of the alphabet, sharing:

    • Name, occupation, family data
    • "Why I am attending this seminar"
    • "One thing I want you to know about me is . . ."

6. Have the participants select "Learning Partners," preferably someone they do not know very well. This is done by asking people to: (1) look around (2) take the initiative in asking the person they have spotted (3) spend a brief time chatting. It wouldn't seem that this method could bring people together as learning partners, but it does. Trust it.
7. Using the introduction as a model, the equipper should tell the participants where he or she is in his or her journey regarding lay people doing pastoring. This honest sharing will help the people be open and honest about where they are. The equipper divides the participants into groups of four, which will include two sets of learning partners, to share with each other where they are in their journey.

The Equipping Units

Unit 1
The Concept of Lay People Pastoring

1. Teach chapter 1.
2. If the number of participants does not exceed 20, remain as a group. If more than 20, divide into groups of six (three sets of learning partners).
3. Read the statement on page 29, "There are lay people like these in every church . . . . "
   a. Identify some of these people in your church and describe their caring actions.
   b. If you are one who is identified, be humbly grateful and accept the affirmation.
4. Ask, "What are your thoughts about the two assumptions on page 31?" Provide time for discussion.
5. Ask, "How much do you believe Samuel Southard's statement on page 33, 'Many persons can do most of what we pastors can do . . . '?" Provide time for planting this concept deeply into the minds and hearts of the people.

Unit 2
The Biblical Basis

Teach chapter 2. Ask selected participants to read the Scripture references as you teach this unit.

Unit 3
Who Needs It?

1. Teach chapter 3.
2. Divide into groups of four (either two sets of learning partners or a random selection) to share: How you have been cared for (pastored) by another. By whom? How? When? And one need which *you,* or a *friend* or your *family* is now experiencing.
3. After all four have shared, pray for one another about these needs. Have each pray for *only* one other person, praying specifically for the shared need.
4. After this experience, the equipper asks, "Do you know what you have just done? (pause) You have pastored one another."
5. Have the total group debrief on how it felt to (1) pray and (2) be prayed for.

Unit 4
What a Lay Pastor Does

1. Teach chapter 5, pages 63-71.
2. Have large letters of PACE displayed, or mount them one at a time as you talk about them. Other ways of accentuating them are to write them on a chalkboard or use an overhead projector.
3. After you have taught the unit, divide into groups of four to discuss:

    a. What you understand PACE to be, knowing that this is the description of what constitutes basic pastoring. (Number off from 1 to 4: 1 takes *P,* 2 takes *A*, 3 takes *C*, and 4 takes *E*.)
    b. Your ability to effectively do all four.
    c. How you feel about reports.

d. What you bring to pastoring. *Examples:* Experience, training, resources, spiritual life, patience, pastoring gifts, etc.

Note: At this point in the seminar you may want to (1) study the lists of spiritual gifts in Romans 12:6-8; 1 Corinthians 12:4-11,28; and 1 Peter 4:8-11; (2) discuss pages 79-81; and/or give the Modified Houts Questionnaire cited on page 85.

Unit 5
Pastoral Supervision

1. Teach chapter 5, pages 71-78.
2. Ask the participants to get with their learning partners. Questions to facilitate supervisory dialogue are in the Addendum, pp. 231-232. (These may be copied and distributed to the participants.) Select one question from the "Personal Self" set of questions. Role-play with one person being the "shepherd," the other being the "lay pastor." The shepherd asks the question that will open the dialogue. Next, reverse roles and take a question from the "Ministering self" category and role-play.
3. Following the role-playing bring the total group together to discuss:

  • how they felt about asking the question
  • how they felt about being asked the question
  • how they feel about being accountable—being "supervised."

Unit 6
Being Professional

1. Teach chapter 7, pages 93-97.
2. Discuss as a total group or in small groups of four (two sets of learning partners) these salient points:

   a. What is the difference between being *a* professional and being professional? Give examples, e.g. the sterile atmosphere of some doctors' offices and some doctors' cold, objective manners.
   b. Do you anticipate any difficulty in "getting down to business" when you become a lay pastor? How will you shift from small talk to more serious talk?

3. Ask the total group to do "word associations": asking them to say the first word or thought that comes to their minds as you call out the following words or phrases.

   - "Authority" (from 5, page 96)
   - "Dependable" (from 6, page 96)
   - "Being Available" (from 7, page 96)
   - "Assertive" (from 8, page 96)
   - "Knowing your limitations" (from 9, page 96)
   - "Forgiving yourself" (from 10, page 97)

   Note: Give time for all who want to make their contribution to do so, but without unnecessary delays.

Unit 7
Being Precedes Doing

1. Teach chapter 7, pages 97-102.
2. Have the learning partners share with each other the two points which they consider the most important and tell why.

Unit 8
Imperatives for Personal Spiritual Health

1. Teach chapter 7, pages 102-107.
2. In groups of four or six (two or three sets of learning partners) have each person share what he or she is doing to keep spiritually healthy. Also, have each share what the hindrances are and what you have done about them. Ask each group to appoint a "reporter" to take notes and report to the whole group.
3. Assemble the whole group to hear the reports. You may expect some creative and usable ideas to be shared.
4. An alternative to the above plan would be to invite a lay person from your church or another church, whom you know has a regular time with the Lord, to tell his or her experiences.
5. Separate into twos (*not* learning partners) to use the Campus Crusade booklet, *How to Be Filled with the Holy Spirit*. To shorten the time required, they can read through the prayer on page 12 and stop. After reading the prayer they should ask each other if they can sincerely make that prayer their own. If so, they should each read it separately and out loud, making it their prayer.

Unit 9
The Anatomy of a Visit

1. Teach chapter 7, pages 107-111.
2. Role-play the phone calls in learning-partner twosomes.
   - Have them determine who is to be the lay pastor and who is to be the flock member.
   - With chairs back-to-back so they cannot see each other, the "lay pastor" calls the "flock member" to make an appointment for the First Visit.

222

- Then turn chairs so the two can face each other. The "visit" is made, incorporating the 12 components listed on pages 108 and 109.
- Reverse the roles and do it again so each benefits from the experience.

3. A video tape of a First Visit is available from CHPC, Lay Pastors Ministry, 5742 Hamilton Avenue, Cincinnati, Ohio 45224 (Phone: 513/541-5676). If this is used, ask the participants prior to viewing the tape to look for the 12 components. After the viewing ask the group to tell which of the 12 they identified. They should critique the effectiveness of what was viewed.

4. The First Visits on pages 110-111 of the book (seven actual visits by a CHPC lay pastor) are to be analyzed in these three ways:

   a. What do these reports tell about the flock members?
   b. What do these reports tell about the lay pastor?
   c. What would you pray about and plan to do next?

The following forms may be copied and used individually by the participants. Each one is to have his or her own copy in order to work separately. When they are finished, their answers can either be shared with the full group and evaluated, or one or two selected individuals can share their answers with the whole group, or the answers can be shared and discussed in small groups.

First Visit Reports

1. What do these reports tell about the flock members?

    1 _____
    _____
    2 _____
    _____
    3 _____
    _____
    4 _____
    _____
    5 _____
    _____
    6 _____
    _____
    7 _____
    _____

2. What do these reports tell about the lay pastor?

    1 _____
    _____
    2 _____
    _____
    3 _____
    _____
    4 _____
    _____
    5 _____
    _____
    6 _____
    _____
    7 _____
    _____

3. If you were the lay pastor who turned in these seven reports, what would you: (1) pray about and (2) plan to do next?

    1 Pray about _____

      Plan to do next _____

    2 Pray about _____

      Plan to do next _____

    3 Pray about _____

      Plan to do next _____

    4 Pray about _____

      Plan to do next _____

    5 Pray about _____

      Plan to do next _____

    6 Pray about _____

      Plan to do next _____

    7 Pray about _____

      Plan to do next _____

Unit 10
Authority to Pastor

Teach chapter 7, pages 112-114.

Unit 11
The Lay Pastor Listens

1. Teach chapter 7, pages 114-119.
2. Divide the participants into groups of three. In each group one will have a *speaker*, a *listener* and an *observer*.
3. The purpose of this laboratory experience is to practice "paraphrasing" (sometimes called "reflective listening"), one of the most simple of the listening skills. *Paraphrasing is the skill of repeating in your own words what you understand the speaker is intending to say.* It also assures the speaker you are interested in what he or she is saying. Example of "paraphrasing":

   Speaker: "My neighbor has deliberately ignored me for the past two weeks."

   Listener (paraphrasing): "Your neighbor has intentionally not spoken to you."

4. Give these instructions:

   a. The *speaker* will talk about anything to the *listener* for three minutes (last Sunday's sermon, what is being learned in the Equipping Seminar, a vacation experience, etc.).
   b. The *listener* paraphrases a few statements during the three minutes to be sure he or she is

226

understanding, and to show his or her interest in what is being said.

   c. The *observer* gives special attention to the *listener* to note how *he* or *she* is doing in the paraphrasing—whether the paraphrasing is helping or hindering the flow of the story.

5. After three minutes the *observer* reports his or her observations to the other two. The three of them, then, discuss the listening experience.
6. This is repeated two more times with each assuming a new role each time so that each has the experience of being *speaker, listener* and *observer*.
7. The total group reassembles and discusses what was learned in the exercise.

Unit 12
Confidentiality

1. Teach chapter 7, pages 119-121.
2. The following questions can be discussed either by the group as a whole or by small groups of four or six (two or three 3 sets of learning partners).

   a. Why is it essential to keep confidential those things told you in private?

   b. What damage is done when confidentiality is broken?

   c. What is the difference between public and private information?

   d. What do you do about the "gray" areas, when it is not clear whether certain information is public or private?

   e. What can you do to build trust in a pastoring relationship so the flock member knows you will keep private matters confidential?

227

Evaluating the Equipping Seminar

To ask the participants to evaluate the seminar is a great help in planning the next one. A sample evaluation form which has been used at CHPC is in the Appendix. These should be distributed to the participants sometime during the last quarter of the seminar with the request to complete and turn them in before leaving. A reminder at the close may be necessary. The planning group will want to get together to evaluate the seminar within a week. This is a good time to begin plans for the next seminar.

Concluding the Seminar

Assemble the group in a circle. Place a candle in the center symbolizing the presence of Jesus. Read Revelation 1:12-18 to accentuate His presence. Join hands. Give opportunity to all who desire to share what the seminar has meant to them. Close with a song and prayer.

Addendum:
Equipping Shepherds

This part of the Leader's Guide is specifically designed to equip shepherds. This material was not included in the book because it is supplemental.

People who are to be shepherds will need additional equipping beyond that which is provided for lay pastors in the book.

The following outline will guide those who equip shepherds.

A. Material from the book:
1. The two roles of shepherds, page 71.
   a. Pastoring
   b. Pastoral supervision
2. Shepherds are a support for the lay pastors, page 72.
   a. appreciation is needed
   b. loneliness, discouragement and anxiety may attack the lay pastor
   c. occupational hazards are:
      (1) loss of motivation
      (2) decline of enthusiasm
      (3) thoughts of quitting
3. The value of the question, "How is your ministry going?" Page 72.
   a. self-evaluation
   b. accountability
   c. spot weaknesses
   d. opportunity to suggest improvements
   e. opens the door for affirming
4. Five steps to focus a pastoring experience, page 72-73.
5. The definition of pastoral supervision, page 73.
   a. What "doing and reflecting on ministry" means
   b. Four ways a pastor will grow in supervision
6. Shepherds are models for lay pastors, page 76.

7. Developing shepherding abilities and behavior, page 77.
B. The shepherd/lay pastor visit.
  1. Covenant together to meet regularly. If this is not done, pastoral supervision is likely to break down—it will not happen.
  2. Set a specific time and place to meet. This should be done monthly, or at least bi-monthly.
  3. Ask the lay pastor to prepare for the visit by thinking about his or her:
    a. Strengths
    b. Ministry successes in the past month (or two months)
    c. Areas of needs and weaknesses they may feel.
  4. Discuss one highlight or problem in detail, remembering to respect the principles of confidentiality.
    NOTE: Occasionally writing a verbatim of one experience will be very helpful.
  5. Either before or after dealing with the person's pastoring ministry, the shepherd will need to direct the conversation to the lay pastor's personal life. Inquiring about how things are going at this time in his or her life will facilitate pastoring. There may be need for personal ministry, affirmation and special prayer at this point. This may be a good time for the shepherd to share what the Lord is doing in his or her life, thus creating the opportunity for mutual ministry.
  6. The following suggestions/questions are useful in facilitating a productive visit.
    a. Personal Self:
       • "Let's talk about some Scriptures which have become meaningful to us since we last visited."

- "I'd like to share with you where I believe I'm growing spiritually/relationally/intellectually/socially."
- "Let's talk about what we are doing currently to keep ourselves close to our Lord."
- "Did you have a good experience at last Sunday's worship service?"
- "How is _____(name of lay pastor)_____?" (Focusing on the person, as opposed to job, family, pastoring, etc.)
- "Tell me about your family."
- "Tell me about your work."

b. Ministering Self:
  - "How do you feel about what you are doing?"
  - "What has been the high point in your pastoring since we last met?"
  - "What kind of problems are you discovering people have?"
  - "Are you finding any difficulties in your pastoring?"
  - "Are there areas where you feel the need for more equipping?"
  - "Do you have plans for additional equipping?"
  - "Are you discovering any new pastoring gifts?"
  - "Do you have suggestions from your experience to pass on to the Ministry Group or Pastoral Staff?"

7. Spend some quality time with the lay pastor in praying over what surfaced in the visit.
8. Help the lay pastor set short-range goals (monthly, weekly or other) for accomplishing his or her ministry.

9. Make out your report soon after leaving the lay pastor.

C. Building and maintaining integrity
   1. Shepherds must do what they say they will do. If an appointment cannot be kept or if they must be late, they must contact the lay pastor to inform and explain. If a commitment is made to a lay pastor to give assistance, contact someone for them, etc., the commitment must be kept. If it becomes impossible to carry through on a commitment the lay pastor must be contacted and other arrangements made. It is imperative that lay pastors are able to say of their shepherds, "They are dependable. They keep their commitments."
   2. Since integrity (being dependable and accountable) is a two-way street, the shepherd assumes responsibility to hold the lay pastor to his or her commitments. If the shepherd does not do this the lay pastor may conclude that:
      a. The shepherd does not care; and/or
      b. The commitment is not important.
      On the other hand, by holding them accountable, the lay pastors will learn that:
      a. They are expected to keep their commitments
      b. What they are doing is so important that if it is not done the church will suffer and
      c. *They* (the lay pastors) are important to the total work of Christ in His Church
      d. They are, in fact, the ministry.
   3. By fulfilling your commitment to hold your lay pastors accountable you are maintaining your integrity and helping them to maintain theirs. Much guilt, remorse, disgust, mediocrity and failure will be avoided by being faithful in this.

D. Shepherds have authority.
   Review this unit with the shepherds since it is the

233

same taught to lay pastors on pages 112-114.

E. Jesus as Supervisor*

1. He was engaged in the ministry in which He invited people to share.
2. He gathered about Him a small group of learners with whom He shared the task of ministry.
3. He met with the disciples to reflect on their common experience.
4. He was one who spoke and acted with an authority based on personhood rather than position.
5. He maintained both intimacy and distance with His disciples.
6. He instructed, corrected, exemplified, chided, loved, supported, challenged and "stuck by" the ones for whom He had accepted responsibility.
7. He entrusted to His learners the ministry with confidence in their ability to get on with the task [and with the promise, "I am with you always"].
8. He gave to those whom He supervised His full authority to do even greater things than He had been able to do.

* From *Pastoral Supervision,* by Kenneth H. Pohly, page 94.

Appendix

The materials contained in this appendix are samples of what is used at CHPC. Feel free to adopt or adapt them for your own use.

Appendix Contents

Lay Pastor Application

Name _____

Telephone _____

Address _____

Married status _____

Number of years member of CHPC _____

Ministries and/or offices held in the past _____

_____

Ministries and/or offices currently held _____

_____

_____

Why I want to be a lay pastor: _____

_____

_____

_____

_____

_____

How I have been equipped for being a lay pastor: _____

_____

_____

Depending on the Holy Spirit:

_____ I confess Jesus Christ to be my Lord and Saviour.

_____ I will minister under the authority of the Session.

_____ I will be faithful in this ministry.

_____ I will seek further equipping as it is available and to the extent I am able.

_____ I will commit myself to continuing personal spiritual growth.

Signed _____

(Spouse sign here if joint ministry)

Date _____

(over)

You may, if you choose, request up to 50 percent of your flock. There is no assurance that your request can be honored but they will be given special consideration.

Names of People I (we) Request:

_____

_____

_____

_____

_____

Lay Pastors Equipping Seminar
College Hill Presbyterian Church

Saturday, July 19, 1986—10:00 A.M. to 9:00 P.M.

10:00-10:30	Getting Acquainted and Worship
10:30-10:40	Video Introduction
10:40-11:00	"Concept and Theology"
11:00-11:15	"The Need"
11:15-11:30	Break
11:30-12:00	"The Call"
12:00-12:30	Groups
12:30-1:30	Lunch
1:30-2:15	"Commitments"
2:15-2:30	Review Commitments (Questions)
2:30-3:00	Groups Re-Commitments
3:00-3:15	Break
3:15-4:45	"The Anatomy of a Visit"
4:45-5:45	First Visit Report Models
5:45-7:00	Free Time and Dinner
7:00-7:45	"Managing Difficulties"
7:45-8:15	"Pastoral Supervision" (Shepherds)
8:15-8:30	Groups (Practice Pastoral Supervision)
8:30-8:45	"Authority to Pastor"
8:45-9:00	Review and Worship

Sunday, July 20, 1986—11:00 A.M. to 4:00 P.M.

11:00-12:30	"The Lay Pastor Listens"
12:30-1:15	Lunch
1:15-1:30	"Being Precedes Doing"
1:30-1:45	"Imperatives for Personal Spiritual Health"
1:45-2:15	"The Holy Spirit in Pastoring"
2:15-2:30	"Being Professional" (Video)
2:30-3:00	Break
3:15-3:45	Applications and Evaluation
3:45-4:00	Closing

"Tend the flock of God that is your charge"

—1 Peter 5:2

Evaluation Paper
Lay Pastors Equipping Seminar

1. The equipping experience met my expectation.
   (Circle the number representing your response)

	low			high	

   —To *know* one another .1 2 3 4 5

   —To learn what a *Lay Pastor does* 1 2 3 4 5

   —To be *equipped* for *basic/minimal*
   pastoring
   (PACE) 1 2 3 4 5

   —To understand the *reason* for our L.P.
   Ministry. 1 2 3 4 5

   —To be *affirmed* in *my call* to be a
   Lay Pastor 1 2 3 4 5

   —To know the *biblical basis* for the
   L.P. Ministry 1 2 3 4 5

2. Rank the 13 sessions 1, 2, or 3 in their order of
   importance as you see them:

   > 1—Very important
   > 2—Important
   > 3—Not so important

   _____ The Concept, Theology and Need of Lay
   Pastoring

   _____ The Call

   _____ Commitments

   _____ The Anatomy of a Visit

   _____ Managing Difficulties

   _____ Pastoral Supervision (Shepherds)

   _____ Authority to Pastor

_____ The Lay Pastor Listens

_____ Being Precedes Doing

_____ Imperatives for Personal Spiritual Health

_____ The Holy Spirit in Pastoring

_____ Being Professional

_____ Confidentiality

3. I would like to have had sessions in these additional areas: _____

_____

_____

4. Some things I suggest you do on the next equipping seminars: _____

_____

_____

5. The effectiveness of the teaching:

   I understood the teaching as presented

	low				high
—The Concept, Theology and Need of Lay Pastoring	1	2	3	4	5
—The Call	1	2	3	4	5
—Commitments	1	2	3	4	5
—The Anatomy of a Visit	1	2	3	4	5

Commissioning of Lay Pastors

People committing themselves to minister as Lay Pastors and approved for pastoring will be commissioned at a special service.

Even though it is not appropriate in the United Presbyterian Church USA to use the word "ordain" in setting people apart to minister as Lay Pastors, the spirit of ordination as Jesus used this term in John 15:16 (KJV) is to characterize their commitment. The Greek word *tithemi,* translated *ordain* means to place, appoint, ordain, set forth.

The term *commission* will be used in setting aside those called forth to minister in College Hill Presbyterian Church as Lay Pastors.

When the time for commissioning comes, the presiding ordained pastor will ask the following questions:

1. Do you trust in Jesus Christ as your Saviour and Lord and acknowledge Him to be head of the church?

2. Do you believe in one God; Father, Son and Holy Spirit?

3. Will you be faithful in the work and worship of this church and diligently seek to grow in the grace and knowledge of Jesus Christ?

4. Will you be a Lay Pastor in obedience to Jesus Christ, guided by the Holy Spirit to the glory of God the Father?

5. Will you minister in Jesus' name under the authority of the Session of this church and subject to the Holy Scriptures?

6. Will you seek to pastor your people faithfully and with love?

The questions having been answered in the affirmative, the Lay Pastors are to be set apart for this ministry by prayer and laying on of hands by the elders. The following declaration will then be made:

"_____, you are now commissioned as a Lay Pastor, to minister as the pastor of a designated flock of College Hill Presbyterian Church members. The grace of the Lord Jesus Christ be with you. Amen."

Report of First Visit

Family _____

                 Initial contact date _____

                 Initial visit date _____

Getting Acquainted

Check list: Phoned for appointment   _____

                Prayed before going   _____

                Small talk   _____

                Explained Lay Pastor Ministry   _____

                Gave blue booklet   _____

                Explained availability   _____

                Gave card   _____

                Made record after returning home   _____

                Am praying for them daily   _____

How you were received: Graciously   _____

                            Reluctantly   _____

                            Not at all   _____

General Evaluation of First Visit _____

_____

_____

Plans for Next Visit _____

_____

_____

Goals for Pastoring (Based on first visit) _____

_____

_____

                              _____

                                Lay Pastor(s)

Lay Pastors Contacts

Lay Pastors Name(s)			Month / Year	

Date	Name	Code	Joys and Concerns When Appropriate (Avoid Confidential Information)	Help!

Contact Code: 1—Home visit
2—Other face-to-face visit
3—Telephone
4—Mail
5—Other (Please explain)

"Help" Code: A—Discussion w/ Shepherd requested
B—Discussion w/ Mel or Marge requested

Shepherd's Name

Note: Please log contacts and mail *white* and *pink* copies to your Shepherd on the 1st of each month.

Shepherd's Contact Report

Shepherd(s) —————————————————— ———————— ————
Month(s) Year

Lay Pastor's Name	Contacts Made Lay Pastor's Effectiveness (circle one)	Contact Dates	Type of Contact
	1 2 3 4 5		
	1 2 3 4 5		
	1 2 3 4 5		
	1 2 3 4 5		
	1 2 3 4 5		
	1 2 3 4 5		
	1 2 3 4 5		
	1 2 3 4 5		
	1 2 3 4 5		
	1 2 3 4 5		
	1 2 3 4 5		
	1 2 3 4 5		
	1 2 3 4 5		
	1 2 3 4 5		

Additional Comments:

Contact code:
1—Home visit
2—Telephone
3—Mail
4—Talked at church
5—Supervisory
6—Other (please explain)

Note: Please turn in bi-monthly to the Pastoral Ministries office.

pink—office copy
white—Shepherd's copy

247

OUR COMMITMENT TO YOU

To pray for you regularly.

To contact you on a regular basis.

To be available to you
whenever/wherever possible.

To provide a Christian example.

MINISTRY CHARGE
1 Peter 5:2-3

LAY
PASTORS
MINISTRY

TEND
THE
FLOCK

THE LAY PASTORS MINISTRY

College Hill Presbyterian Church

Serving you in His Name
as your Lay Pastor

_____

_____

TELEPHONE _____

Lay Pastors Visit Evaluation

We are asking you to call on each family in your flock between now and May 3. Then, complete this form and turn it in to the Pastoral Ministries office (Mel's or Marge's desk) by May 3. Do not take this form into the home with you. Fill it out after the visit.

I. Pastoral Contacts

A. Family #_____ (One form is provided for each family in your flock. Please do not identify by name.)
Date of visit _____ Length of visit _____
Number in family _____
Number at home during visit _____

B. Visit Activity (Check those performed)
_____ Friendly chit-chat (small talk)
_____ Talked about church
_____ Talked of problems or needs
_____ Encouraged or affirmed them
_____ Shared my (our) faith
_____ Prayed
_____ Read Scripture
_____ Other _____

C. Other kinds of contacts made since January 1:
_____ Card
_____ Phone
_____ Casual, at church
_____ Unplanned, at the store, etc.
_____ Other _____

II. Feelings About the Visit

A. My (our) inner feeling about the visit before going:

Hot _____ Warm _____ Cold _____

B. My (our) inner feeling about the visit after making it:

Super _____ Good _____ Fair _____ Badly _____

III. Pastoral Relationships

On a scale of 1 to 10 circle the number which most closely indicates how *you* see *your* relationship.

	(Hot)									(Cold)
Single Person	1	2	3	4	5	6	7	8	9	10
Husband	1	2	3	4	5	6	7	8	9	10
Wife	1	2	3	4	5	6	7	8	9	10
Child #1	1	2	3	4	5	6	7	8	9	10
Child #2	1	2	3	4	5	6	7	8	9	10
Child #3	1	2	3	4	5	6	7	8	9	10
Other Household										
Members #1	1	2	3	4	5	6	7	8	9	10
Members #2	1	2	3	4	5	6	7	8	9	10
Members #3	1	2	3	4	5	6	7	8	9	10

Lay Pastors Total Ministry Evaluation

I. The Pastoring Person(s)

A. I (we) pray for our people:

Daily _____ Weekly _____ Occasionally _____ Never
_____

B. Why I (we) am/are pastoring:

(Check all statements that apply)

_____ People need it
_____ God called me to do it
_____ I feel good about doing it
_____ I am growing by doing it
_____ I don't know why I am doing it
_____ Other _____

C. Awareness of spiritual state:

Pastors need to know where their people are spiritually if they are to minister effectively. On the scale of 1 to 10 circle the number which indicates the extent of *your* awareness of *their* spiritual state.*

1   2   3   4   5   6   7   8   9   10
Fully aware   No awareness

* Keep in mind how aware you are of their depth of commitment to Christ, their walk with the Lord, their growth in the knowledge of Scripture, etc.

D. My (our) current level of commitment to pastoring.

On a scale of 1 to 10 circle the number indicating *your* perception of *your* level of commitment.

1   2   3   4   5   6   7   8   9   10
None   Deep

II. Pastoring Data

A. An estimate of number of hours spent in pastoring my people ____

B. I (we) could pastor additional families (circle the appropriate number).   1   2   3   4   5

C. An estimate of number of miles traveled since January 1 in pastoral activity ____

D. The monthly "Shepherd's Call" is interesting and helpful.

____ agree   ____ disagree   ____ undecided

I (we) read it

____ Never   ____ Frequently   ____ Occasionally   ____ Regularly

E. My (our) estimate of the quarterly "Lay Pastors Fellowship"
____ of no importance
____ of little importance
____ fairly important
____ very important

F. How well do I know my shepherd?
____ very well
____ somewhat
____ I do not have a shepherd

G. My (our) feeling about making out the monthly report
____ willing and doing it
____ willing but not doing it
____ reluctant but doing it
____ reluctant and not doing it
____ resistant but doing it
____ resistant and not doing it
____ do not know what it is

III. Additional Equipping

A. How adequate do you believe you are equipped to pastor?

____ very well   ____ quite well   ____ partially
____ not at all

B. How open are you to receiving more equipping?

____ Open but do not have time
____ Open; have plans for additional equipping
____ Open; will welcome counsel on what to do
____ Not open

Signed _____

Date _____

Lay Pastors Ministry Evaluation
(To be given to people being pastored.)

1. We believe a person/family is pastored when loved, visited, prayed for, helped, confronted, listened to, nurtured and encouraged. On a scale of 1 to 10, how well do you feel you are being pastored? *(Circle one number in each row)*

	Low									High
Loved	1	2	3	4	5	6	7	8	9	10
Visited	1	2	3	4	5	6	7	8	9	10
Prayed for	1	2	3	4	5	6	7	8	9	10
Helped	1	2	3	4	5	6	7	8	9	10
Confronted	1	2	3	4	5	6	7	8	9	10
Listened to	1	2	3	4	5	6	7	8	9	10
Nurtured	1	2	3	4	5	6	7	8	9	10
Encouraged	1	2	3	4	5	6	7	8	9	10

2. Contacts from your lay pastor might be a personal visit, a letter or card, a phone call, etc. *(check the appropriate statements)*

   _____ There *were* more contacts at the beginning than now.

   _____ There *are* more contacts *now* than at the beginning.

   _____ Contacts have been on a regular frequency since the beginning.

   _____ Contacts have *never* been on a regular frequency.

3. I would like to see my lay pastor: (check one)
   _____ more _____ less _____ not at all _____ just right the way it is

4. We believe in mutual ministry, that a flock member can minister to his/her lay pastor as well as the lay pastor ministering to you. I have ministered to my lay pastor:

_____ some   _____ none   _____ a lot

5. The best thing my lay pastor has done for me is _____
_____
_____

6. The relationship between me/us and my/our Lay Pastor(s):
   (Check appropriate line(s).)

_____ has deepened _____ has declined _____ never developed

_____ is good   _____ (other) _____

7. Influence on our Christian life is from several sources. *Please circle one number in each row*, which best describes the impact the following sources have had on your spiritual life.

	Low								High	
Senior Pastor	1	2	3	4	5	6	7	8	9	10
Other Staff	1	2	3	4	5	6	7	8	9	10
Lay Pastor	1	2	3	4	5	6	7	8	9	10
Radio-T.V.	1	2	3	4	5	6	7	8	9	10
Books and Magazines	1	2	3	4	5	6	7	8	9	10

Neighbors   1   2   3   4   5   6   7   8   9   10

Other
Churches   1   2   3   4   5   6   7   8   9   10

8. I would like to be a Lay Pastor:

_____ never   _____ sometime   _____ now*

9. I want to say this about the Lay Pastors Ministry in CHPC:

_____

_____

_____

_____

_____

_____

_____

* Please contact Dr. Mel Steinbron or Marge Miller (542-5676) or write your name on this form so one of us can contact you to tell you how you can become a lay pastor.

The Three Levels of Equipping Lay Pastors

The purpose of equipping is to help Lay Pastors build a relationship which will enable them to minister in times of need and earn the right to facilitate maturity in Christ. The purpose of the three levels of equipping is to give Lay Pastors the opportunity to intentionally mature over a period of time in their pastoring confidence and effectiveness.

Level I

Building the Pastoral Relationship. (John 15:12,13)

1. Equipping Seminar
   P—Pray daily. Close contact will help to pray right.
   A—Affirm availability. This can be done during the regular contacts. Asking for prayer requests is one way to affirm availability.
   C—Contact regularly.
      —a minimum of one contact per month by phone, mail, at church, etc.
      —a minimum of two home visits a year.
      —special attention in time of sickness, crisis or death.
      —special attention in celebration time: birthdays, anniversaries, holidays, graduations, births, promotions, etc.
   E—Be an example. The example will be seen and understood in the contacts. (Phil. 3:17; 1 Tim. 4:12; 1 Peter 5:3)

2. On-the-job Training (1 or more home visits with veteran Lay Pastor following the Equipping Seminar and prior to being commissioned.)

Level II

Pastoring in Times of Need. (Matt. 25:35)

1. Equipping Provisions

   a. Stephen Series
   b. Apples of Gold, I & II
   c. Rational Christian Thinking
   d. Gary Collins' tapes with supervision
   e. Electives from CLA

2. Requirements: Apples of Gold I and II, Stephen Series, plus 2 others of your choice.

Level III

Facilitating Maturity in Christ (Col. 1:28)

1. Equipping Provisions

   a. HELPER Clinic
   b. Counseling with Power Seminar
   c. Dare to Care Seminar
   d. ABC's of Growing in Christ (or similar CLA class)

2. Requirements: All of the above four.

Strong communication in the Lay Pastors Ministry is vital. For a sample copy of "The Shepherd's Call" newsletter, sent by CHPC to all lay pastors in their program, write College Hill Presbyterian Church, 5742 Hamilton Avenue, Cincinnati, Ohio 45224.